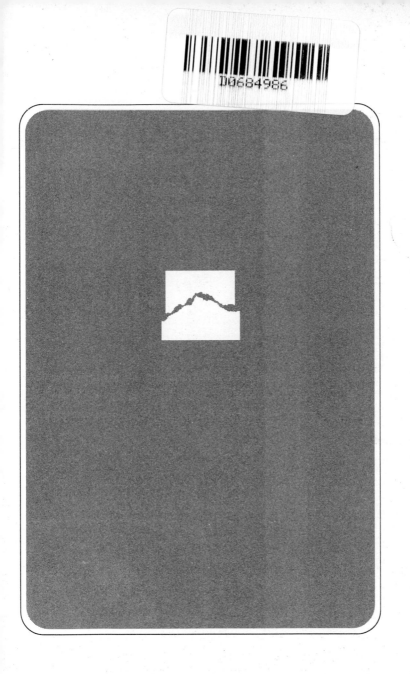

Compiled by
Susan Besze Wallace

Foreword by Julie Newmar

THE SUMMIT GROUP

Arlington, Texas

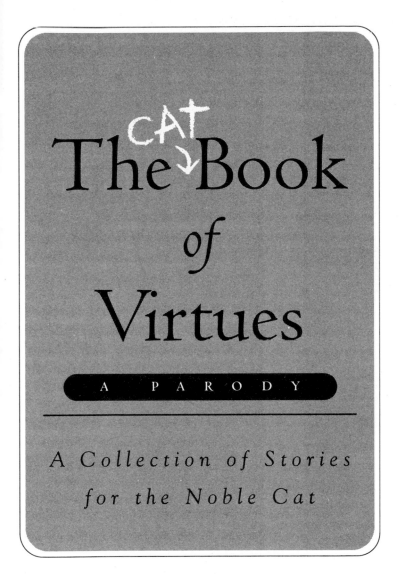

The ~~cat~~ Book of Virtues

A PARODY

A Collection of Stories
for the Noble Cat

THE SUMMIT GROUP
One Arlington Center
1112 East Copeland Road
Suite 510
Arlington, Texas 76011

Cover illustration by Gorland Mar

Printed in the United States of America
99 98 97 96   030   2 3 4 5 6

Library of Congress Cataloging-in-Publication Data
The cat book of virtues, a parody: a collection of stories for the noble cat / edited by
    Susan Besze Wallace.
        p.cm.
    Includes bibliographical references.
    ISBN 1-56530-168-4 (pbk.)
    1. Cats—Literary collections. I. Wallace, Susan Besze, 1969-
PN6071.C3C32 1995
808.8'036—dc20

                                                                        95-6074
                                                                        CIP

To Todd and Samantha,
this girl's best friends.

Table of Contents

Foreword

The circuitry connecting Stanley Ralph Ross's brain to his fingertips flows with pure genius. He wrote five of the six episodes in which I appeared as Catwoman on the *Batman* television series of the sixties, sleekly dressed head to toe in skintight black as the stealthy arch-nemesis to the Caped Crusader. Stanley was to Gotham City what Shakespeare was to historical Europe: In Stanley's case, his words provided high-octane fuel for Catwoman's prima donna role. They never clogged the engine. Instead, his scripts energized me to be felinely arrogant, susurrant of voice, and lithely pompous. The dancer's bits were mine: Little choreographic diagrams would appear in my script, much like the drawing boards used by directors in illustrating scenes for cameramen, art directors, and assistant directors.

To me, the funniest scenes included my sidekicks, those unruly and flatly incompetent blokes. Catwoman's companions in crime unwittingly sabotaged her schemes, rendering her something less than all-powerful, although still seething with self-assurance. Opposites attract—and make for heavenly comedy.

Naturally, every female cat is six feet tall, physically unchallenged, and in possession of special sartorial secrets. Whatever curious popularity I have as a performer is usually ascribed to my being "larger than life." In truth, it has been my ability to "right-size" myself that has defined me as a woman during the changing eras of American culture. In the fifties and early sixties, I recall bending at the knees so that the male star could look me in the eye. Other times, I sugar-coated my voice to lend fragility and vulnerability to my femininity. These early acting efforts now look dated. It was the Catwoman role that ultimately provided for me the benchmark transition between eras.

In the Cat world, it is the female who decides which male has his pleasure with her. I've noticed that men don't mind—in fact, they enjoy—being dominated, provided the results are mainly pleasurable. Incidentally, Desmond Morris's book *Catwatching* was my resource for the film *Oblivion*, in which I played the madam of an outer-space cathouse. Director Sam Irwin insisted I was a cat in an earlier life. Maybe, maybe not. But I often wonder why I am always asked to purr—on street corners, in television studios, and at restaurant tables. You tell me.

It is true that all the cats I've played have a background that includes ballet school. It's all in the feline choreography of living and loving: the quietest room, the softest pillow, when and where the sun's rays are kindest, who keeps the tidbits, and which trees offer the most frolic and the fastest escape. The perfect earthly dancer—the cat.

> —Julie Newmar
> *TV's Catwoman and*
> *real-life companion to four cats*

Introduction

There is, indeed, no single quality of the cat that man could not emulate to his advantage.

Carl Van Vechten (1880-1964)

Oh, the lessons we could learn.

For nearly four thousand years, the cat has been a source of great fascination, tremendous admiration—and considerable consternation. But ailurophile or ailurophobe, one must admit the cat has qualities from which humans could benefit.

Narrowing the list of cat virtues, trying to include the most universal in a single volume, created more than a little dismay. A cat's individual nature assured that not every cat lover's favorite trait could be represented. At the risk of leaving out characteristics of importance, I have composed a list of nine common virtues. These are illustrated in celebration of the feline mystique.

The literature that exists probing the cat's persona is as diverse as the animal itself. From Edgar Allen Poe's horror story *The Black Cat* to Mother Goose's nonsense rhymes, the lessons in cat character are a mix of the familiar, the frank, the funny, even the frivolous. In fables and folklore, poetry and prose, the cat's idiosyncrasies have been noted for centuries.

Cat aficionados range from Anne Frank, whose pet Mouschi provided loyal companionship as she hid with her family from Nazis, to Mark Twain, a lifelong cat lover who kept up to eleven at once—and wrote about nearly as many. These famed feline fans have explored a virtue or two of the cat in their own unique way.

This book was written not to educate readers on the virtuous, righteous, or noble character of cats, but to celebrate their inscrutable, enigmatic nature. Hopefully, in the process, this collection will broaden the perspective of those who have yet to have a cat grace their lives. Enjoy.

1

Independence

Cats don't need like other animals need.

They do not bound to greet their arriving owner. They do not need a door opened when they hear the call of nature. They clean themselves. They entertain themselves.

Cats are selective about the company they keep—and when they keep it. Such self-reliance makes sometimes perfect, sometimes unlikely pets. Cat lovers are not lonely. Instead, they relish sharing their homes with a creature who complements their existence, without constantly tugging at it.

You never own a cat—you exist with him. Some take this to mean the cat is an arrogant, aloof animal, though it is doubtful anyone who has ever lived with a cat would say such a thing. Sure, some cats are a bit bigheaded, but so are some of us, and we don't label the entire human race stuck-up.

The cat's independent and individual nature does have a more tangible downfall—large, unwanted litters of kittens. Many a telephone pole and bus stop sport signs announcing "Free Kittens," the sad result of cat self-sufficiency that often leads to owner neglect.

The happier side of independence solidifies its status as a virtue of the cat. There are all sorts of tales of "lost" cats who spend days, even weeks, wandering the city or traversing state lines, only to appear back home, safe and healthy. Their wanderlust is wondrous. Their independence, admirable.

from Love is a Happy Cat

Michael W. Fox

Love is
respecting
the fact that
some
independent
felines just
don't take
to being
cuddled.

Love is realizing
that a cat is a cat
—a creature with
idiosyncrasies
to be enjoyed
and understood,
not controlled
or dominated.

Love is appreciating
the paradoxical
nature of cats:
we love whom
we choose, and we
are dependent
upon no one.

Give me liberty, or give me death.

A cat from Virginia

"A Cat's Conscience"

Anonymous

Cats are never accompanied by thoughts of regret.

A dog will often steal a bone,
But conscience lets him not alone,
And by his tail his guilt is known.

But cats consider theft a game,
And, howsoever you may blame,
Refuse the slightest sign of shame.

When food mysteriously goes,
The chances are that Pussy knows
More than she leads you to suppose.

And hence there is no need for you,
If Puss declines a meal or two,
To feel her pulse and make ado.

The cat lives alone, has no need of society, obeys only when she pleases, pretends to sleep that she may see the more clearly and scratches everything on which she can lay her paw.

François-Auguste-René de Chateaubriand
(1768-1848)

"Kitten's Night Thoughts"

Oliver Herford (1863-1935)

Cats are even resourceful in their independence.

When Human Folk put out the light
And think they've made it dark as night,
A Pussy Cat sees every bit
As well as when the lights are lit.

When Human Folk have gone upstairs
And shed their skins and said their prayers,
And there is no one to annoy,
Then Pussy may her life enjoy.

No human hands to pinch or slap,
Or rub her fur against the nap,
Or throw cold water from a pail,
Or make a handle of her tail.

And so you will not think it wrong,
When she can play the whole night long,
With no one to disturb her play,
That Pussy goes to bed by day.

———————

Socks Clinton, unlike Madonna, did absolutely nothing to attract the world's attention. Furthermore, he will continue to do absolutely nothing. If guests at the White House hope to see him, he'll probably hide. Anyone who expects him to be cute on command has never met a cat.

Despite his adoptive family's determined efforts to shield him from the press, Socks Clinton will stay famous all the time Chelsea Clinton's father is in office. Nonetheless, his will remain a cat's life: snoozing followed by eating followed by snoozing followed by pushing corks across the kitchen floor. At times he may be impelled to claw the leg of a chair. But he will never have to claw his way to the top.

New York Times *editorial*

———————

Look at the stray cat
Sleeping . . . snug under the eaves
In the whistling snow.

Taigi (d. 1771)

"Cats"

A. S. J. Tessimond (1902-1962)

Cats, like many men, don't feel the need to ask for directions. They just go.

Cats, no less liquid than their shadows,
Offer no angles to the wind,
They slip, diminished, neat, through loopholes
Less than themselves; will not be pinned

To rules or routes for journeys; counter
Attack with non-resistance; twist
Enticing through the curving fingers
And leave an angered, empty fist.

They wait, obsequious as darkness,
Quick to retire, quick to return;
Admit no aims or ethics; flatter
With reservations; will not learn

To answer to their names; are seldom
Truly owned till shot and skinned.
Cats, no less liquid than their shadows,
Offer no angles to the wind.

It may have been noticed that I use the word "guardianship," in preference to "ownership," of a cat. "Ownership" implies authority over body and soul. A dog, in its devotion, will of its own free will accept this authority; a cat, never.

Marguerite Steen

---

from Guiness's Animal Facts and Feats

Gerald L. Wood

In 1948, Mincha, a black female cat, ran up a forty-foot tree in Buenos Aires, Argentina, never to climb down to humans again. Food was stretched to her by pole, thanks to the locals. She lived in the treetop six years—and even delivered six lots of kittens there.

"Cat"

Mary Britton Miller

The black cat yawns,
Opens her jaws,
Stretches her legs,
And shows her claws.

Then she gets up
and stands on four
Long stiff legs
And yawns some more.

She shows her sharp teeth,
She stretches her lip,
Her slice of a tongue
Turns up at the tip.

Lifting herself
On her delicate toes,
She arches her back
As high as it goes.

She lets herself down
With particular care,
And pads away
With her tail in the air.

Cats are absolute individuals, with their own ideas about everything, including the people they own.

John Dingman

––––––––

"The Cat and Mouse in Partnership"

The Brothers Grimm

A cat's independence is sometimes severe enough to sever friendships.

A cat, having made acquaintance with a mouse, professed such great love and friendship for her that the mouse at last agreed that they should live and keep house together.

"We must make provision for the winter," said the cat, "or we shall suffer hunger. And you, little mouse, must not stir out, or you will be caught in a trap."

So they took counsel together and bought a little pot of fat. Then they could not tell where to put it for safety, but after long consideration the cat said there could not be a better place than the church, for nobody would steal there. And they decided to put it under the altar and not touch it until they were really in want. So the little pot was placed in safety. But before long the cat was seized with a great desire to taste it.

"Listen to me, little mouse," said he. "I have been asked by my cousin to stand godfather to a little son she has brought into the world. He is white with brown spots, and they want to have the christening today. So let me go to it, and you stay at home and keep house."

"Oh yes, certainly," answered the mouse. "Pray go, by all means. And when you are feasting on all the good things, think of me. I should so like a drop of the sweet red wine."

But there was not a word of truth in all this. The cat had no cousin and had not been asked to stand godfather. He went to the church, straight up to the little pot, and licked the fat off the top. Then he took a walk over the roofs of the town, saw his acquaintances, stretched himself in the sun, and licked his whiskers as often as he thought of the little pot of fat. And then when it was evening he went home.

"Here you are at last," said the mouse. "I expect you have had a merry time."

"Oh, pretty well," answered the cat.

"And what name did you give the child?" asked the mouse.

"Top-off," answered the cat dryly.

"Top-off!" cried the mouse. "That is a singular and wonderful name. Is it common in your family?"

"What does it matter?" said the cat. "It's not any worse than Crumb-picker, like your godchild."

A little time after this the cat was again seized with a longing for the pot of fat.

"Again I must ask you," said he to the mouse, "to do me a favor and keep house alone for a day. I have been asked a second time to stand godfather, and as the little one has a white ring round its neck, I cannot well refuse."

So the kind little mouse consented, and the cat crept along by the town wall until he reached the church, where he went straight to the little pot of fat and ate half of it.

"Nothing tastes so well as what one keeps to oneself," said he, feeling quite content with his day's work. When he reached home, the mouse asked what name had been given to the child.

"Half-gone," answered the cat.

"Half-gone!" cried the mouse. "I never heard such a name in my life. I'll bet it's not to be found in the calendar."

Soon after that the cat's mouth began to water again for the fat.

"Good things always come in threes," said he to the mouse. "Again I have been asked to stand godfather. The little one is quite black with white feet, and not any white hair on its body. Such a thing does not happen every day, so you will let me go, won't you?"

"Top-off, Half-gone," murmured the mouse. "They are such curious names, I cannot but wonder at them."

"That's because you are always sitting at home," said the cat, "in your little gray frock and hairy tail, never seeing the world, and fancying all sorts of things."

So the little mouse cleaned up the house and set it all in order. Meanwhile the greedy cat went and made an end of the little pot of fat.

"Now all is finished, one's mind will be easy," said he, and came home in the evening quite sleek and comfortable. The mouse asked at once what name had been given to the third child.

"It won't please you any better than the others," answered the cat. "It is called All-gone."

"All-gone!" cried the mouse. "What an unheard-of name! I never met with anything like it. All-gone! Whatever can it mean?" And shaking her head, she curled herself round and went to sleep. After that the cat was not again asked to stand godfather.

When the winter had come and there was nothing more to be had out of doors, the mouse began to think of their store.

"Come, cat," said she, "we will fetch our pot of fat. How good it will taste, to be sure!"

"Of course it will," said the cat. "Just as good as if you stuck your tongue out of the window."

So they set out, and when they reached the place they found the pot, but it was standing empty.

"Oh, now I know what it all meant," cried the mouse. "Now I see what sort of partner you have been! Instead of standing godfather you have eaten it all up. First Top-off! Then Half-gone! Then—"

"Hold your tongue!" screamed the cat. "Another word, and I eat you too!"

And the poor little mouse, having "All-gone" on her tongue, out it came, and the cat leaped upon her and made an end of her. And that is the way of the world.

Two cats in one bag cannot have peace.

Yiddish proverb

"Pangur Bán"

Anonymous

In the eighth century, a monastery student in Corinthia wrote this poem on a copy of St. Paul's Epistles. His independence, and his cat's, proved a pleasant mix.

I and Pangur Bán, my cat,
'Tis a like task we are at:
Hunting mice is his delight,
Hunting words I sit all night.

Better far than praise of men
'Tis to sit with book and pen;
Pangur bears me no ill-will,
He too plies his simple skill.

'Tis a merry thing to see
At our tasks how glad are we,
When at home we sit and find
Entertainment to our mind.

Oftentimes a mouse will stray
In the hero Pangur's way;
Oftentimes my keen thought set
Takes a meaning in its net.

'Gainst the wall he sets his eye
Full and fierce and sharp and sly;

'Gainst the wall of knowledge I
All my little wisdom try.

When a mouse darts from its den,
O how glad is Pangur then!
O what gladness do I prove
When I solve the doubts I love!

So in peace our tasks we ply,
Pangur Bán, my cat, and I;
In our arts we find our bliss,
I have mine and he has his.

Practice every day has made
Pangur perfect in his trade;
I get wisdom day and night
Turning darkness into light.

———————

from "The Suicidal Cat"

Anonymous

Gloriously out of step, not a care in the world, a cat's
independence has its price, though often, it's priceless.

There was a man named Ferguson,
He lived on Market Street,
He had a speckled Thomas cat

That couldn't well be beat;
That cat could catch more mice, and sich,
Than forty cats could eat.

This cat would come into the room
And climb upon a cheer,
And there he'd set and lick hisself,
And purr so awful queer,
That Ferguson would yell at him—
But still he'd purr—severe.

And then he's climb the moonlit fence,
And loaf around and yowl,
And spit and claw another cat
Alongside of the jowl;
And then they both would shake their tails
And jump around and howl.

Oh, this here cat of Ferguson's
Was fearful then to see;
He'd yell precisely like he was
In awful agony;
You'd think a first-class stomach-ache
Had struck some small baby.

And all the mothers of the street,
Waked by the horrid din,
Would rise right up and search their babes
To find some worrying pin;
And still this viperous cat would keep
A-hollerin' like sin.

And as for Mr. Ferguson,
'Twas more than he could bear,
And so he hurled his bootjack out
Right through the midnight air;
But this vociferous Thomas cat
Not one cent did he care.

For still he yowled and kept his fur
A-standin' up on end,
And his old spine a-doublin' up
As far as it would bend,
As if his hopes of happiness
Did on his lungs depend.

"The Kilkenny Cats"

Mother Goose

There were once two cats of Kilkenny.
Each thought there was wan cat too many;
So they fought and they fit,
And they scratched and they bit,
Till, excepting their nails,
And the tips of their tails,
Instead of two cats, there weren't any.

2

Perseverance

I once watched a kitten spend an hour playing with two cotton balls. Now, that's perseverance. Have you ever seen a cat give himself a bath? He meticulously licks every square inch of fur, slowly, deliberately, precisely. Nothing gets in the way.

Perseverance marks everything a cat does: playing, eating, grooming, stalking, seeking attention. Many a cat lover begins each day aware of this feline quality, awakened as they are by a cat's paws treading over their sheets or fur rubbing against their cheeks.

Though the cat's sticktuitiveness is usually a virtue, it can be his undoing. This was the case with the puss of eighteenth-century writer Thomas Gray, so intent on a tub of goldfish:

> Presumptuous Maid! with looks intent
> Again she stretched, again she bent,
> Nor knew the gulf between.
> (Malignant Fate sat by and smiled.)
> The slippery verge her feet beguiled,
> She tumbled headlong in.

A few daring writers have used the word "dumb" to describe cats who get themselves in these situations. Perhaps the term is used affectionately, but still I can't submit. I envy the cat's concentration, giving singular attention to whatever task is at hand. People, always trying to do too many things at once, should take note. Besides, perseverance is surely the reason cats can be potty trained—and the reason their homes are mouse-free!

from The Tiger
in the House

Carl Van Vechten (1880-1964)

She wants her breakfast at a certain hour in the morning; if the door of my bedroom is closed she gives little cries outside. If it is open she enters, puts her forepaws on the edge of my bed close to my face and licks my cheek. If I brush her away, in a few moments she is nibbling my toes. I put an end to this and very shortly she is marching up and down, using me as a highroad. She is equally persistent if I am taking a nap. On such occasions she often climbs high on my breast and sleeps with me, but when she awakes she digs her claws into my chest and stretches, quite as if I didn't exist. This alternate protrusion of the forepaws, with toes separated, as if pushing against and sucking their mother's teats, is a favourite gesture of cats when they are pleased.

"Cat Jeoffry"

Christopher Smart (1722-1771)

During Smart's four years in a London madhouse, Jeoffry
was his only friend. They persevered together, as shown in
this most revered passage.

For I will consider my Cat Jeoffry.

For he is the servant of the Living God, duly and daily serv-
ing him.

For at the first glance of the glory of God in the East he
worships in his way.

For this is done by wreathing his body seven times round
with elegant quickness.

For then he leaps up to catch the musk, which is the blessing
of God upon his prayer.

For he rolls upon prank to work it in.

For having done duty and received blessing he begins to consider himself.

For this he performs in ten degrees.

For first he looks upon his forepaws to see if they are clean.

For secondly he kicks up behind to clear away there.

For thirdly he works it upon stretch with the forepaws
extended.

For fourthly he sharpens his paws with wood.

For fifthly he washes himself.

For sixthly he rolls upon wash.

For seventhly he fleas himself, that he may not be interrupted
upon the beat.

For eighthly he rubs himself against a post.

For ninthly he looks up for his instructions.

For tenthly he goes in quest of food.

For having consider'd God and himself he will consider his
neighbour.

For if he meets another cat he will kiss her in kindness.

For when he takes his prey he plays with it to give it a
chance.

For one mouse in seven escapes by his dallying.

For when his day's work is done his business more properly
begins.

For he keeps the Lord's watch in the night against the
adversary.

For he counteracts the powers of darkness by his electrical
skin and glaring eyes.

For he counteracts the Devil, who is death, by brisking about
the life.

For in the morning orisons he loves the sun and the sun
loves him.

For he is of the tribe of Tiger.

For the Cherub Cat is a term of the Angel Tiger.

For he has the subtlety and hissing of a serpent, which in
goodness he suppresses.

For he will not do destruction, if he is well-fed, neither will
he spit without provocation.

For he purrs in thankfulness, when God tells him he's a
good Cat.

For he is an instrument for the children to learn benevolence
upon.

For every house is incompleat without him and a blessing is
lacking in the spirit.

For the Lord commanded Moses concerning the cats at the
    departure of the Children of Israel from Egypt.
For every family had one cat at least in the bag.
For the English Cats are the best in Europe.
For he is the cleanest in the use of his forepaws of any
    quadrupede.
For the dexterity of this defense is an instance of the love of
    God to him exceedingly.
For he is the quickest to his mark of any creature.
For he is tenacious of his point.
For he is a mixture of gravity and waggery.
For he knows that God is his Saviour.
For there is nothing sweeter than his peace when at rest.
For there is nothing brisker than his life when in motion.
For he is of the Lord's poor, and so indeed is he called by
    benevolence perpetually—Poor Jeoffry! poor Jeoffry!
    the rat has bit thy throat.
For I bless the name of the Lord Jesus that Jeoffry is better.
For the divine spirit comes about his body to sustain it in
    compleat cat.
For his tongue is exceeding pure so that it has in purity what
    it wants in musick.
For he is docile and can learn certain things.
For he can set up with gravity which is patience upon
    approbation.
For he can fetch and carry, which is patience in employment.
For he can jump over a stick which is patience upon proof
    positive.
For he can spraggle upon waggle at the word of command.
For he can jump from an eminence into his master's bosom.
For he can catch the cork and toss it again.

For he is hated by the hypocrite and miser.

For the former is afraid of detection.

For the latter refuses the charge.

For he camels his back to bear the first motion of business.

For he is good to think on, if a man would express himself neatly.

For he made a great figure in Egypt for his signal services.

For he killed the Icneumon-rat very pernicious by land.

For his ears are so acute that they sting again.

For from this proceeds the passing quickness of his attention.

For by stroking of him I have found out electricity.

For I perceived God's light about him both wax and fire.

For the electrical fire is the spiritual substance, which God sends from heaven to sustain the bodies both of man and beast.

For God has blessed him in the variety of his movements.

For, tho' he cannot fly, he is an excellent clamberer.

For his motions upon the face of the earth are more than any other quadrupede.

For he can tread to all the measures upon the musick.

For he can swim for life.

For he can creep.

It is, of course, totally pointless to call a cat when it is intent on the chase. They are deaf to the interruptive nonsense of humans. They are on cat business, totally serious and involved.

John D. MacDonald

from A letter to son Kermit, January 6, 1903

Theodore Roosevelt

A dose of presidential perseverance.

Tom Quartz is certainly the cunningest kitten I have ever seen. He is always playing pranks on Jack and I get very nervous lest Jack should grow too irritated. The other evening they were both in the library—Jack sleeping before the fire—Tom Quartz scampering about, an exceedingly playful little creature— which is about what he is. He would race across the floor, then jump upon the curtain or play with the tassle. Suddenly he spied Jack and galloped to him. Jack, looking exceedingly sullen and shame-faced, jumped out of the way and got upon the sofa and around the table, and Tom Quartz instantly jumped upon him again. Jack suddenly shifted to the other sofa, where Tom Quartz again went after him. Then Jack started for the door, while Tom made a rapid turn under the sofa and around the table and just as Jack reached the door leaped on his hind- quarters. Jack bounded forward and away and the two went tandem out of the room—Jack not cooperating at all; and about five minutes afterwards Tom Quartz stalked solemnly back.

Six little mice sat down to spin;
Pussy passed by and she peeped in.
What are you doing, my little men?

Weaving coats for gentlemen.
Shall I come in and cut off your threads?
No, no, Mistress Pussy, you'd bite off our heads.
Oh, no, I'll not; I'll help you to spin.
That may be so, but you can't come in.
Says Puss: You look so wondrous wise,
I like your whiskers and bright black eyes;
Your house is the nicest house I see;
I think there is room for you and for me.
The mice were so pleased that they opened the door,
And Pussy soon had them all dead on the floor.

Mother Goose

————————

The Lion and the Cat

Appearances can be deceiving. Perseverance can over-
come seemingly impossible obstacles.

A great lion lay fast asleep in the woods. A kitten came
along, a little teeny, tiny kitten. The kitten thought the
sleeping lion was a big pile of dried grass, he was lying so still.
So the kitten began scampering up and down on the beast.

"Gr—!" growled the lion. The kitten's little feet tickled
the lion's stomach. Tickle, tickle. The lion wriggled and
growled some more, and then opened one of his giant eyes.
He saw the annoying little kitten and reached out and
grabbed him by the tail.

"So it's you!" he roared. "I'll stop you yet, you persistent little kitty!" And he picked up the kitten by the tail.

The little animal was quite frightened. His heart skipped a few beats, but he purred: "O Great King of Beasts, please don't hurt me! I'll never forget the kindness if you spare me this once!"

A sly grin spread over the fierce lion's lips, and he swung the kitten back and forth by his tail.

The kitten shuddered, and got dizzy. "Please let me go, please! Who knows, great King, if you let me go maybe someday I could be helpful to you!"

"You help *me*?" scoffed the lion. "A teeny thing like you help the King of Beasts? Ha!"

He laughed so long and so hard that he made himself feel pretty happy.

"Well, you're really too small an animal for me to bother with . . ." And he opened his paw and the kitten fell to the ground with a thud and ran away.

Not too long after this encounter, the lion fell into a hole left by hunters who wanted to catch him and carry him to their king, caged forevermore. The lion moaned in the hole and the hunters saw their prey. They pulled him out and tied him to a tree while they went to get a wagon.

The lion tugged and tugged but could not get free. "I'll never see this forest again," he lamented. As he cried and sighed, the tiny kitten happened by.

"Well, well, I see the King of Beasts is in quite a spot," teased the kitten.

"The hunters have got me," the lion said sadly, "and there's not a thing I can do about it."

"Is that all?" the kitty asked.

"You needn't be so flippant about it," the lion said. "It's a very sad day for me!"

But the kitty had already approached the rope that held the lion and began to use his sharp little claws, the same claws that persisted in annoying the lion, to free the beast.

It took hours, and the kitten grew tired, but as it is with cats, he persevered. Eventually, the rope split and began to break. Tear, tear, snip, snip. And finally, the lion was free.

"You said I could never help you, but what's truer is that I never give up," said the kitten. "I have set you free."

"Well, well," said the lion. "Look what you've done. A tiny thing like you. I'm ashamed that I ever doubted your size, or the strength of your intentions. Good-bye little friend. And thank you!"

———

Min caught a mouse, and was playing with it in the yard. It had got away from her once or twice and she had caught it again, and now it was stealing off again, as she was complacently watching it with her paws tucked under her, when her friend, Riorden, a stout cock, stepped up inquisitively, looked down at the mouse with one eye, turning its head, then picked it up by the tail, gave it two or three whacks on the ground, and giving it a dexterous toss in the air, caught the mouse in its open mouth. It went, head foremost and alive, down Riorden's capacious throat in the twinkling of an eye, never again to be seen in this world; Min all the while, with paws comfortably tucked under her, looked on unconcerned. What did one mouse matter, more or less, to her? The cock walked off amid the currant-bushes, stretched his neck up and gulped once or twice, and the deed was accomplished. It might be set down among the *Gesta gallorum*. There were several human witnesses. It is a question whether Min ever understood where that mouse went to. She sits composedly sentinel, with paws tucked under her, a good part of her days at present, by some ridiculous little hole, the possible entry of a mouse.

Henry David Thoreau (1817-1862)

from "Last Words to a Dumb Friend" (1904)

Thomas Hardy (1840-1928)

Perseverance is not always pretty, but it is usually respected.

Pet was never mourned as you,
Purrer of the spotless hue,
Plumy tail, and wistful gaze,
While you humoured our queer ways,
Or outshrilled your morning call
Up the stairs and through the hall—
Foot suspended in its fall—
While, expectant, you would stand
Arched, to meet the stroking hand;
Till your way you chose to wend
Yonder, to your tragic end.

From the chair whereon he sat
Sweep his fur, nor wince thereat;
Rake his little pathways out
Mid the bushes roundabout;
Smooth away his talons' mark
From the claw-worn pine-tree bark,
Where he climbed as dusk enbrowned
Waiting us who loitered round.

Strange it is this speechless thing,
Subject to our mastering,
Subject for his life and food
To our gift, and time, and mood;
Timid pensioner of us Powers,
His existence rules by ours,
Should—by crossing at a breath
Into safe and shielded death,
By the merely taking hence
Of his insignificance—
Loom as largened to the sense,
Shape as part, above man's will,
Of the Imperturbable.

3

Intelligence

Most cat owners are predisposed to think their animal is smart. Generally speaking, they're correct. The cat's IQ is superior to that of most dogs—and many other animals. Cats learn by observing others; monkeys and chimpanzees are believed to be the only other animals to do that.

But the range of the cat's intelligence goes far beyond laboratory experiments and escape-from-the-box tests. Cats also have common sense. They are sometimes cunning, usually coy. Throughout literature we see cats think first and act second, calculating every move. Humans who do that are called sensible, while such a cat is labeled devious.

Cats are smart enough to know what they have to do to get what they want. Purring is one way they do this most effectively. Charles Darwin observed, "Cats use their voices much as a means of expression, and they utter under various emotions and desires at least six or seven different sounds. The purr of satisfaction, which is made during both inspiration and expiration, is one of the most curious."

Curiosity is a sure sign of the cat's intelligence. Never bored, they find fascination and creative play wherever they are. And yet "the cat seldom interferes with other people's rights," says Carl Van Vechten. "His intelligence keeps him from doing many of the foolish things that complicate life."

A cat is nobody's fool.

Heywood Broun (1888-1939)

———

Ah! cats are a mysterious kind of folk. There is more passing in their minds than we are aware of. It comes no doubt from their being too familiar with warlocks and witches.

Sir Walter Scott, whose cat's name was Hinse
(1771-1832)

———

"The Cat and the Fox"

Aesop

True intelligence beats any amount of bragging. Cats talk the talk and walk the walk.

A fox was boasting to a cat one day about how clever he was. "Why, I have a whole bag of tricks," he bragged. "I know at least a hundred different ways of escaping my enemies, the dogs."

"How remarkable," said the cat. "I have only one trick, though I usually make it work. I wish you could teach me some of yours."

"Well, sometime when I have nothing else to do," said the fox, "I might teach you one or two of my easier ones."

Just at that moment they heard the yelping of a pack of hounds coming straight toward the spot where they stood. Quickly the cat scampered up a tree and disappeared in the leaves. "This is the trick I told you about," she called down to the fox. "Which one are you going to use?"

The fox sat there trying to decide which of his many tricks he was going to employ. Nearer and nearer came the hounds. When it was already too late, the fox decided to run for it. But even before he started, the dogs were upon him, and that was the end of the fox.

Moral: One good plan that works is better than a hundred doubtful ones.

Notebook, 1895

Mark Twain

A cat is more intelligent than people believe, and can be taught any crime.

Cats are smarter than dogs. You can't get eight cats to pull a sled.

Jeff Valdez

"Little Robin Redbreast Sat upon a Tree"

Mother Goose (c. 1760)

Cats play their hands close to the vest, never showing more cards than necessary.

Little Robin Redbreast sat upon a tree,
Up went the Pussy-cat, and down went he,
Down came Pussy-cat, away Robin ran;
Says little Robin Redbreast: "Catch me if you can!"

Little Robin Redbreast jumped upon a spade,
Pussy-cat jumped after him, and then he was afraid.
Little Robin chirped and sang, and what did Pussy say?
Pussy-cat said: "Mew, mew, mew," and Robin flew away.

———

"Puss in Boots," 1696

Charles Perrault

This delightful, historical tale is the quintessential story on cat smarts.

There was a miller who left no more estate to the three sons he had than his mill, his ass, and his cat. The partition was soon made. Neither scrivener nor attorney was sent for. They would soon have eaten up all the poor patrimony. The eldest had the mill, the second the ass, and the youngest nothing but the cat. The poor young fellow was quite comfortless at having so poor a lot.

"My brothers," said he, "may get their living handsomely enough by joining their stocks together; but for my part, when I have eaten up my cat and made me a muff of his skin, I must die of hunger."

The cat, who heard all this, but made as if he did not, said to him with a grave and serious air:

"Do not thus afflict yourself, my good master. Your fortunes are not so bad as you seem to think. You do not value me highly enough. You need only give me a bag and get a pair of boots made for me that I may scamper through the dirt and the brambles, and you shall see that you have not so bad a portion of me as you imagine."

The cat's master did not build very much upon what he said. He had often seen him play a great many cunning tricks to catch rats and mice, as when he used to hang by the heels, or hide himself in the meal, and make as if he were dead; so that he did not altogether despair of his affording him some help in his miserable condition. When the cat had what he asked for, he booted himself very gallantly, and putting his bag about his neck, he held the strings of it in his two fore paws and went into a warren where there was a great abundance of rabbits. He put bran and sow-thistle into his bag, and stretching out at length, as if he had been dead, he waited for some young rabbits, not yet acquainted with the deceits of the world, to come and rummage his bag for what he had put into it.

Scarce was he lain down but he had what he wanted. Two rash and foolish young rabbits jumped into his bag, and

Monsieur Puss, immediately drawing close the strings, took them away without pity. Proud of his prey, he went with it to the palace and asked to speak with his majesty. He was shown upstairs into the King's apartment, and making a low reverence, said to him:

"I have brought you, sire, two rabbits of the warren, which my noble lord the Marquis of Carabas (for that was the title which Puss was pleased to give his master) has commanded me to present to your majesty from him."

"Tell your master," said the King, "that I thank him and that he does me a great deal of pleasure."

Another time he went and hid himself among some standing corn, holding still his bag open, and when a brace of partridges ran into it, he drew the strings and so caught them both. He went and made a present of these to the King, as he had done before of the rabbits which he took in the warren. The King, in like manner, received the partridges with great pleasure and ordered him some money for drink.

The cat continued for two of three months thus to carry his majesty, from time to time, game of his master's taking. One day in particular, when he knew for certain that he was to take the air along the riverside with his daughter, the most beautiful princess in the world, he said to his master:

"If you will follow my advice your fortune is made. You need only go and wash yourself in the river, in that part I shall show you, and leave the rest to me."

The Marquis of Carabas did what the cat advised him to, without knowing why or wherefore. While he was washing the King passed by, and the cat began to cry out:

"Help! help! My Lord Marquis of Carabas is going to be drowned."

At this noise the King put his head out of the coach-window, finding it was the cat who had so often brought him such good game, he commanded his guards to run immediately to the assistance of his lordship the Marquis of Carabas. While they were drawing the poor marquis out of the river, the cat came up to the coach and told the King that while his master was washing there came by some rogues, who went off with his clothes, though he had cried out "Thieves! thieves!" several times as loud as he could.

This cunning cat had hidden them under a great stone. The King immediately commanded the officers of his wardrobe to run and fetch one of his best suits for the Marquis of Carabas.

The King caressed him after a very extraordinary manner, and as the fine clothes he had given him extremely set off his good mien (for he was well-built and very handsome in his person), the King's daughter took a secret inclination to him, and the Marquis of Carabas had no sooner cast two or three respectful and somewhat tender glances but she fell in love with him to distraction. The King would needs have him come into the coach and take part of the airing. The cat, quite overjoyed to see his project begin to succeed, marched on before, and meeting with some countrymen who were mowing in a meadow, he said to them:

"Good people, you who are mowing, if you do not tell the King that the meadow you mow belongs to my Lord Marquis of Carabas, you shall be chopped as fine as herbs for the pot."

The King did not fail to ask of the mowers to whom the meadow they were mowing belonged.

"To my Lord Marquis of Carabas," they answered all together, for the cat's threats had made them terribly afraid.

"This," said the marquis, "is a meadow which never fails to yield a plentiful harvest every year."

The master cat, who went still on before, met with some reapers and said to them:

"Good people, you who are reaping, if you do not tell the King that all this corn belongs to the Marquis of Carabas, you shall be chopped as fine as herbs for the pot."

The King, who passed by a moment after, would needs know to whom all that corn did belong.

"To my Lord Marquis of Carabas," replied the reapers, and the King was very well pleased with it, as well as with the marquis, whom he congratulated thereupon. The master cat, who went always before, said the same words to all he met, and the King was astonished at the vast estates of my Lord Marquis of Carabas. Lord Monsieur Puss came at last to a stately castle, the master of which was an ogre, the richest that had ever been known; for all the lands which the king had then gone over belonged to this castle. The cat, who had taken care to inform himself who this ogre was and what he could do, asked to speak with him, saying he could not pass so near his castle without having the honor of paying his respects to him.

The ogre admitted him and made him sit down.

"I have been assured," said the cat, "that you have the gift of being able to change yourself into all sorts of creatures you have a mind to. You can, for example, transform yourself into a lion, or an elephant."

"That is true," answered the ogre very briskly; "and to convince you, you shall see me now become a lion."

Puss was so sadly terrified at the sight of a lion so near him that he cried out loudly, and would have run away had not the ogre quickly resumed his natural form. However, he owned he had been very much frightened.

"I have been moreover informed," said the cat, "but I know not how to believe it, that you have also the power to take on you the shape of the smallest animals; for example, to change yourself into a rat or a mouse. But I must own to you I take this to be impossible."

"Impossible!" cried the ogre. "You shall see that presently."

And at the same time he changed himself into a mouse and began to run about the floor. Puss no sooner perceived this but he fell upon him and ate him up.

Meanwhile the King, who saw, as he passed, this fine castle of the ogre's, noted its beauty and marveled at its size and grandeur. He had a mind to go into it, and ordered his coach to be driven up to the entrance. Puss, who heard the noise of his majesty's coach running over the drawbridge, ran out and said to the King:

"Your majesty is welcome to this castle of my Lord Marquis of Carabas."

"What! my Lord Marquis," cried the King, "and does this castle also belong to you? There can be nothing finer than this court and all the stately buildings which surround it. Let us go into it, if you please."

The marquis gave his hand to the princess and followed the King, who went first. They passed into a spacious hall, where they found a magnificent collation, which the ogre had prepared for his friends who were that very day to visit him but dared not enter, knowing the King was there. His majesty was perfectly charmed with the good qualities of my Lord Marquis of Carabas, as was his daughter, who had fallen violently in love with him, and seeing the vast estate he possessed, said to him, after having drunk five or six glasses:

"It will be owing to yourself only, my Lord Marquis, if you are not my son-in-law."

The marquis, making several low bows, accepted the honor which his majesty conferred upon him, and forthwith that very same day, married the princess.

Puss became a great lord and never ran after mice any more but only for his diversion.

I've met many thinkers and many cats, but the wisdom of cats is infinitely superior.

Hippolyte Taine (1828-1893)

---

from Essays, II, 1580

Michel de Montaigne

When I am playing with my cat, who knows whether she has more sport in dallying with me, than I have in gaming with her? We entertain one another with mutual apish tricks. If I have my hour to begin or refuse, so hath she hers.

"Two Little Kittens"

Anonymous

True intelligence means knowing when to say when.

Two little kittens, one stormy night,
Began to quarrel and then to fight;
One had a mouse, the other had none,
And that was the way the quarrel begun.

"I'll have that mouse!" said the bigger cat;
"You'll have that mouse? We'll see about that."
"I will have that mouse," said the older one;
"You shan't have that mouse," said the little one.

I told you before 'twas a stormy night
When these two little kittens began to fight;
The old woman seized her sweeping broom
And swept the two kittens right out of the room.

The ground was covered with frost and snow,
And the two little kittens had nowhere to go;
So they lay them down on the mat at the door,
While the angry woman was sweeping the floor

And then they crept in as quiet as mice,
All wet with snow and as cold as ice,
For they found it was better, that stormy night,
To lie down and sleep than to quarrel and fight.

Godey's Lady's Book
May 1895

It is indeed remarkable how much these animals can be taught if taken in kittenhood and treated gently. Even as soon as their eyes open, they can be made to understand many things. . . .

———

Anyone who has ever known a cat really well feels that this cat is superior to most Harvard professors in brain power.

Gladys Tabor

4

Resilience

An indomitable spirit, a physical and spiritual strength, set cats apart from all other animals.

When humans falter, we are told to pick ourselves up, dust ourselves off, and start again. Cats never get down. Should they fall, they land on their feet. They fight but are never knocked out. They run for miles—but who's ever seen one panting or drooling, or dragging its tongue along the ground?

When I was a little girl, my neighborhood was a frenzy of felines. Many had homes, many did not. Often at night I would awaken to cats crooning—followed by clawing, screeching, and finally, more crooning. The screeching unnerved me—like the cry of a baby in pain—and I was always too daunted to look. The next morning, in a flower bed of flourishing cactus plants beneath my window, I would find tufts of cat hair clinging to the spikes. When I myself was unfortunate enough to come in contact with those plants, one sticker brought tears to my eyes. But not those cats. They'd always come back—often the next night. Nine lives, indeed.

Casper, a cat from Willenhall, central England, earned the name Robocat in 1994 after six operations and seventy visits to the veterinarian in two years. After the four-year-old tomcat was found paralyzed in a gutter, thanks to a fight with a fox, steel rods were inserted from his neck to his tail, and held in place with eight bolts.

Writers, philosophers, and even presidents have remarked on the cat's ability to bounce back. President Bill Clinton and his wife Hillary, despite their allergies, allow daughter Chelsea to keep a cat in the White House. Perhaps that adaptability is something they learned from the First Feline, Socks.

From the snow white Angora to the one-eyed alley cat, felines brave discipline, loneliness, and neglect, without missing a beat. On average, cats live fifteen years, though one cat in Great Britain reportedly lived to be thirty-six! Since one year for a cat is the equivalent of about fifteen people years, a cat who lives to be fourteen is 210 in human years. If only we could age so gracefully!

In a world ruled by fad and fancy, staying power is truly a virtue.

No matter how much cats fight,
there always seem to be plenty of kittens.

> *Abraham Lincoln (1809-1865)*
> *He kept four cats in the White House.*

The cat has nine lives: three for playing, three for straying, three for staying.

> *English proverb*

"To Mrs. Reynolds' Cat"

John Keats (1795-1821)

Cats wear their battle scars proudly.

Cat! who hast pass'd thy grand climacteric,
How many mice and rats hast in thy days
Destroy'd?—How many tit-bits stolen? Gaze
With those bright languid segments green, and prick
Those velvet ears—but pr'ythee do not stick
Thy latent talons in me—and upraise
Thy gentle mew—and tell me all thy frays
Of fish and mice, and rats and tender chick.
Nay, look not down, nor lick thy dainty wrists—
For all the wheezy asthma—and for all
Thy tail's tip is nick'd off—and though the fists
Of many a maid have given thee many a maul,
Still is that fur as soft as when the lists
In youth thou enter'dst on glass bottled wall.

————

So Tiberius might have sat,
Had Tiberius been a cat.

Matthew Arnold (1822-1888)

"The Cat of Cats"

William Brighty Rands (1823-1882)

I am the cat of cats. I am
The everlasting cat!
Cunning, and old, and sleek as jam,
The everlasting cat!

————

The cat is the only animal without visible means of support who still manages to find a living in the city.

Carl Van Vechten (1880-1964)

————

from Guiness's Animal Facts and Feats

Gerald L. Wood

An unnamed cat survived three months without food and water in a crate with car parts in Durban, Natal, South Africa, in 1955.

Peter, a three-year-old cat, lived eight days in the underwater cabin of a boat that sank in the Rhine River in 1964.

A cat named Quincy survived falling 180 feet out a nineteenth-story balcony in Canada in 1973.

A kitten sustained fifty-three hours entombed by construction workers in a concrete wall in Skopje, Yugoslavia, in 1974.

A scrawny, blue-eyed, black cat traveled about six thousand miles and spent more than three weeks at sea in the corner of a container being shipped from Taiwan to a warehouse in Mount Vernon, Washington, in March 1994.

Associated Press

Throw a cat over a house and it will land on its feet.

English Proverb

from Romeo and Juliet, III, I

Fortunately for their constituents, royalty isn't as everlasting as the cat.

What wouldst thou have with me?
Good king of cats, nothing but one of your nine lives.

———————

Tomcat Thumb

Come rain, snow, sleet, and hail, even the smallest cats prevail.

A poor cat sat one evening with his wife, howling at the moon. He said, "It's so sad that we don't have any kittens. It's so quiet around here. All our friends' homes are so full of life and fun and laughter."

"Even if it were only one, and if it were no bigger than my thumb, I should be quite content," answered his wife. "We would love it with all our hearts."

Some time after this, she had a little kitten who was strong and healthy, but was no bigger than a thumb. "Well, our wish is fulfilled, and we will love him dearly," they said. And because of his tiny stature, they called him Tomcat Thumb.

He was spoiled with love, but he grew no bigger. Still, he looked out on the world with intelligent eyes, and proved to be smart and spunky and of good fortune.

One day when father cat was getting ready to go mouse hunting he said, "It sure would be nice if I had someone to bring the basket after me."

"Oh, Father," said Tomcat Thumb, "I will bring it. I'll be there right on time."

His father laughed. "You are too small to hold even the handle!"

"That doesn't matter," said Tomcat. "I will get Mother to put it on the wagon and start me rolling down the hill. I can steer from inside."

Tomcat did just as he said, and it happens that as he was rolling along, two men spied the basket that was seemingly steering itself.

"There is something very strange going on," one man said to the other.

The men followed the rolling basket into the woods. Tomcat, seeing his father trolling for mice, called out to his father to stop the wagon.

"You see," Tomcat said, crawling out of the basket, "I told you I could do it, Father!"

The men, watching from behind a tree, were shocked at the tiny cat.

"People in town would pay for just a glance at this little handful," one man said.

And so they approached the father cat. "Sell us your little son. We'll take good care of him."

"No," said the father. "He is my pride and joy and I wouldn't sell him for any amount of gold."

Tomcat perched himself near his father's ear and said, "Father, let me go. I'll come back soon."

So his father handed him over, and the men handed him a thick, shiny piece of gold.

"Where would you like to sit?" the men asked.

"Just put me on your hat," Tomcat said. "Then I can see everyone and everything without getting squished."

Tomcat said good-bye to his father and the trio was off. They walked until the sun began to set. Tomcat told the men to set him down.

When the man took his hat off, Tomcat began to run around in the trees and then jumped in a mousehole.

"Farewell, men. You can go home now," he teased.

The men ran around and poked sticks into the mousehole, but it was no use. Tomcat was tucked into a little nook they could not reach. The angry men started home when it got dark, with no little treasure and no gold.

When they were gone, Tomcat snuck out of his little hiding place. He walked a little, but sensing the danger in the darkness, he crawled into a snail shell he had found, hoping to sleep. Soon after he drifted off, he was awakened by two robbers.

"How shall we steal the parson's gold and silver," one was asking the other.

"I know how," interrupted Tomcat.

"What was that?" one robber asked nervously, looking around. "I heard someone speak."

They stood, rigid and silent.

"Take me along and I'll help," said Tomcat.

"Who are you? Where are you?" they asked.

"Just look on the ground," Tomcat said.

They found him at last and one man put him in the palm of his hand. "How in the world could a little miniature cat help us?"

"I can creep past the iron bars in the pastor's room and hand you what you want," Tomcat explained.

"Well, we can try," the robbers decided. And when they came to the parsonage, Tomcat crept through the bars.

Then, with all his might, he called out, "Do you want everything that is here?"

"SHHHHHH!" hissed the robbers. "Don't wake anyone."

Tomcat pretended not to understand.

"What do you want? Everything?" he shouted again.

The cook heard, and jolted upright in bed. The thieves, now a bit scared, backed up.

"This little cat is just a tease," they thought, starting back.

"Now stop this foolery and hand us something," one robber said.

Tomcat shouted as loud as he could, "I will give you everything, just hold out your hands."

The maid, listening intently like the cook, jumped out of bed and ran to the door. The robbers had fled with the fury of a mouse being chased by a cat. The maid couldn't see anything in the dark, and went to get a light. By the time she got back, Tomcat had slipped out and into the barn. Thinking they must have been dreaming, the maid and the cook went back to bed. Tomcat found a place to sleep in some hay in the barn, and drifted off to dream about returning to his parents.

The maid rose at daybreak to feed the cows. She pulled up an armful of hay—the very hay Tomcat Thumb was resting in. He was sleeping so deeply that he didn't wake until he was nearly in the cow's mouth.

"How did I ever get into this mess?" he exclaimed. Like it or not, and to keep from being chewed up, he had to go down the cow's throat.

"What dreary little quarters. No windows in this house, and hay keeps on pouring in," he lamented.

At last he cried out, "No more food. Please, please, no more food!"

The maid, who was milking the cow, was so shocked she fell off her stool. She ran to get the pastor, but he thought she was losing her mind. When he walked her back to the barn, Tomcat called out again, "Don't give me any more food!"

The pastor was scared, too, and thought the cow was possessed by an evil spirit. He ordered it killed. When it was slaughtered, the stomach was thrown into a manure heap. But by the time Tomcat Thumb began working his way out, a hungry wolf ran by and engulfed the whole stomach with one bite. Still, Tomcat did not lose courage.

"Mr. Wolf," the tiny cat called out, "I know where you can get a grand meal."

"Where would that be?" the wolf inquired.

"Why, in a fine house, where you could squeeze into a storeroom window and find cake and bacon and sausages . . . all you could eat," Tomcat described his father's home.

The wolf grew hungrier with each word, and followed Tomcat's directions. He ate and ate and ate, and in fact he ate so much that he could not return the same way he had entered.

Realizing this, Tomcat began to whoop and holler with all his might.

"Stop!" pleaded the bloated wolf. "You'll wake everyone."

But that was Tom's plan. And soon his parents heard the commotion and came to investigate. His father grabbed an ax when he saw the wolf.

"Dear Father, it's me!" cried Tomcat. "I'm inside the wolf!"

Overjoyed to hear his son's voice, father cat struck the wolf one deadly blow to the head. Then he took a knife to the wolf and set his tiny son free.

"We have been so worried," he cried. "Where have you been?"

"Down a mousehole, in a cow's stomach, and in a wolf's maw," Tomcat answered. "Now I will stay put with you."

"You may be small, but you are more resilient, more strong-willed than creatures a hundred times your size," his parents said, licking and mewing over their only offspring.

"But we will never again sell you for all the riches in the world. For we are wealthy just having your spirit."

Never was a cat or dog drowned
that could see the shore.

Italian Proverb

Curiosity killed the cat, but satisfaction brought it back.

5

Dignity

Wouldn't *you* behave like an aristocrat if *your* ancestors had been worshiped?

Today's domestic cats seem to know that their forefathers were prayed to, embalmed, and enshrined in ancient Egypt, and that virtually every Egyptian house displayed a small cat statue. Cats are always proud, sometimes pompous, and incredibly confident.

There is an air of sophistication in the way they conduct themselves. Countless times, I've witnessed Cotton, a graceful, seemingly benign cat in my neighborhood, stare down dogs five times her size. An obvious physical disadvantage doesn't bother her. She sits motionless, undisturbed by fierce barking that makes neighboring humans want to run for cover.

How cats *refuse* to conduct themselves also says a lot. They do not retrieve balls, bring in newspapers, or roll over and play dead for their owners' amusement. This is due, in part, to these caretakers, who often treat them like the royalty they once were, and give them such monikers as Princess or Precious or Caesar. Some cats have even resided on Capitol Hill, sharing offices with members of Congress.

Cats are privy to extravagant grooming, gourmet food, designer water, and, in some cases, their own bedrooms. One of my friend's kinglike cats, Sinbad, refuses to eat in the company of the other cats who share his home. His food is served in whatever area he finds most comfortable.

Sinbad, like many cats, acts as if he is the ruler of the house. These domestic animals clearly are related to that larger, majestic cat, the king of the jungle.

"The Cat"

Lytton Strachey (1880-1932)

A cat's dignity is apparent from the way he carries his tail and sizes you up with his eyes.

Dear creature by the fire a-purr,
Strange idol eminently bland,
Miraculous puss! As o'er your fur
I trail a negligible hand,

And gaze into your gazing eyes,
And wonder in a demi-dream
What mystery it is that lies
Behind those slits that glare and gleam,

An exquisite enchantment falls
About the portals of my sense;
Meandering through enormous halls
I breathe luxurious frankincense,

An ampler air, a warmer June
Enfold me, and my wondering eye

Salutes a more imperial moon
Throned in a more resplendent sky

Than ever knew this northern shore.
O, strange! For you are with me too,
And I who am a cat once more
Follow the woman that was you.

With tail erect and pompous march,
The proudest puss that ever trod,
Through many a grove, 'neath many an arch,
Impenetrable as a god,

Down many an alabaster flight
Of broad and cedar-shaded stairs,
While over us the elaborate night
Mysteriously gleams and glares!

This passage is one of the most elegant literary capsules describing the cat's dignified demeanor.

I love cats because I love my home, and little by little they become its visible soul. A kind of active silence emanates from these furry beasts who appear deaf to order, to appeals, to reproaches, and who move in a completely royal authority through the network of our acts, retaining only those that intrigue or comfort them.

Jean Cocteau

Rainy afternoon . . .
Little daughter you will never
Teach that cat to dance.

Issa (1763-1827)

In the middle of a world that has always been a bit mad, the cat walks with confidence.

Rosanne Amberson
Twentieth Century writer

"Cats Are Smarter Than Dogs"

from Cat Tales

Sara Pitzer

Deepest apologies to dog lovers, but it's hard to deny the differences.

You can't get six cats to pull a sled.

No cat will keep fetching a ball and returning it to you if all you're going to do is toss it away again.

Your cat won't bark at the UPS man when he's delivering Christmas boxes from your rich aunt, get you fined by nipping at the meter reader, or do something dumb when he realizes that the bookmobile is going to park in front of your house all afternoon.

What self-respecting cat would permit itself to be clipped and groomed like a poodle, with little ruffs around its ankles and all the hair shaved off its body?

A cat refuses to roll over and play dead when she isn't really.

You can't get a cat to stand up and beg for a greasy scrap from your dinner plate. If there's anything there that she wants, she'll just take it. If the scraps are below grade, she'll do without.

Cats won't run races for people to bet on.

No cat would answer to a dumb name like Fido.

---

from an interview in People magazine

Garfield creator Jim Davis

One reason Garfield is interesting for cat lovers is that he confirms what they've always suspected about cats. In Garfield they see his human aspects—his refusal to diet, his inability to walk through a room without knocking things over, and his total pursuit of warm places to curl up and sleep. He champions a lot of unpopular causes, like anti-jogging, and what's more, he doesn't apologize for them.

The Cat Emperor's
New Clothes

When the going gets tough, the tough hold their tails high.

Many years ago there was a Cat Emperor who was so excessively fond of new clothes that he spent all his money on them. He cared nothing about his soldiers, nor for the theater, nor for driving in the woods except for the sake of showing off his new clothes. He had a costume for every hour in the day. Instead of saying as one does about any other king or emperor, "He is in his council chamber," the cats here always said, "The Cat Emperor is in his dressing room." Life was very gay in the great town where he lived. Hosts of strangers came to visit it every day, and among them one day were two swindlers. They gave themselves out as weavers and said that they knew how to weave the most beautiful fabrics imaginable. Not only were the colors and patterns unusually fine, but the clothes that were made of this cloth had the peculiar quality of becoming invisible to every person who was not fit for the office he held, or who was impossibly dull.

"Those must be splendid clothes," thought the Cat Emperor. "By wearing them I should be able to discover which cats in my kingdom are unfitted for their posts. I shall distinguish the wise men from the fools. Yes, I certainly must order some of that stuff to be woven for me."

The Cat Emperor paid the two swindlers a lot of money in advance, so that they might begin their work at once.

They did put up two looms and pretended to weave, but they had nothing whatever upon their shuttles. At the outset they asked for a quantity of the finest silk and the purest gold thread, all of which they put into their own bags while they worked away at the empty looms far into the night.

"I should like to know how those weavers are getting on with their cloth," thought the Cat Emperor, but he felt a little queer when he reflected that anyone who was stupid or unfit for his post would not be able to see it. He certainly thought that he need have no fears for himself, but still he thought he would send somebody else first to see how it was getting on. Every cat in the town knew what wonderful power the stuff possessed, and everyone was anxious to see how stupid his neighbor was.

"I will send my faithful old minister to the weavers," thought the Cat Emperor. "He will be best able to see how the stuff looks, for he is a clever cat and no one fulfills his duties better than he does."

So the good old minister, a tomcat, went into the room where the two swindlers sat working at the empty loom.

"Heaven help us," thought the old minister, opening his eyes very wide. "Why, I can't see a thing!" But he took care not to say so.

Both the swindlers begged him to be good enough to step a little nearer, and asked if he did not think it a good pattern and beautiful coloring. They pointed to the empty loom. The poor old tomcat minister stared as hard as he could, but he could not see anything, for of course there was nothing to see.

"Good heavens," thought he. "Is it possible that I am a fool? I have never thought so, and nobody must know it. Am I not fit for my post? It will never do to say that I cannot see the stuff."

"Well, sir, you don't say anything about the stuff," said the one who was pretending to weave.

"Oh, it is beautiful—quite charming," said the old tom-cat minister, looking through his spectacles and arching his tail high. "Such a pattern and such colors! I will certainly tell the Cat Emperor that the stuff pleases me very much."

"We are delighted to hear you say so," said the swindlers, and then they named all the colors and described the peculiar pattern. The old tomcat minister paid great attention to what they said, so as to be able to repeat it when he got home to the Cat Emperor.

Then the swindlers went on to demand more money, more silk, and more gold, to be able to proceed with the weaving. But they put it all into their own pockets. Not a single strand was ever put into the loom, but they went on as before, weaving at the empty loom.

The Cat Emperor soon sent another faithful official to see how the stuff was getting on and if it would soon be ready. The same thing happened to him as to the old tomcat minister. The official, a Siamese with extraordinary vision, looked and looked, but as there was only the empty loom, he could see nothing at all.

"Is not this a beautiful piece of stuff?" said both the swindlers, showing and explaining the beautiful pattern and colors which were not there to be seen.

"I know I am no fool," thought the Siamese, "so it must be that I am unfit for my good post. It is very strange, though. However, one must not let it appear." So he praised the stuff he did not see, and assured them of his delight in the beautiful colors and the originality of the design.

"It is absolutely charming," he said to the Cat Emperor. Everybody in the town was talking about this splendid stuff.

Now the Cat Emperor thought he would like to see it while it was still on the loom. So, accompanied by a number of selected courtiers, among whom were the two faithful officials who had already seen the imaginary stuff, he went to visit the crafty impostors, who were working away as hard as ever they could at the empty loom.

"It is magnificent," said both the honest officials. "Only see, Your Majesty, what a design! What colors!" And they pointed to the empty loom, for they each thought no doubt the others could see the stuff.

"What?" thought the Cat Emperor. "I see nothing at all. This is terrible! Am I a fool? Am I not fit to be Emperor? Why, nothing worse could happen to me!"

"Oh, it is beautiful," said the Cat Emperor. "It has my highest approval." And he nodded his satisfaction as he gazed at the empty loom. Nothing would induce him to say that he could not see anything.

The whole suite gazed and gazed, but saw nothing more than all the others. However, they all exclaimed with His Majesty, "It is very beautiful." And they advised him to wear a suit made of this wonderful cloth on the occasion of a great procession which was just about to take place. "Magnificent! Gorgeous! Excellent!" went from mouth to mouth. They were all equally delighted with it. The Cat Emperor gave each of the rogues an order of knighthood to be worn in their buttonholes and the title of "Gentleman Weaver."

The swindlers sat up the whole night before the day on which the procession was to take place, burning sixteen candles, so that people might see how anxious they were to get the Cat Emperor's new clothes ready. They pretended to take the stuff off the loom. They cut it out in the air with a huge pair of scissors, and they stitched away with needles without any thread in them.

At last they said, "Now the Cat Emperor's new clothes are ready."

The Cat Emperor with his grandest cat courtiers went to them himself, and both swindlers raised one arm in the air, as if they were holding something. They said, "See, these are the trousers. This is the coat. Here is the mantle," and so on. "It is as light as a spider's web. One might think one had nothing on, but that is the very beauty of it."

"Yes," said all the cat courtiers, but they could not see anything, for there was nothing to see.

"Will Your Imperial Cat Majesty be graciously pleased to take off your clothes?" said the impostors. "Then we may put on the new ones, along here before the great mirror."

The Cat Emperor took off all his clothes, and the impostors pretended to give him one article of dress after the other of the new ones which they had pretended to make. They pretended to fasten something around his waist and to tie on something. This was the train, and the Cat Emperor turned round and round in front of the mirror.

"How well his Majesty looks in the new clothes! How becoming they are!" cried all the cats around. "What a design, and what colors! They are most gorgeous robes."

"The canopy is waiting outside which is to be carried over Your Majesty in the procession," said the master of the ceremonies.

"Well, I am quite ready," said the Cat Emperor. "Don't the clothes fit well?"

Then he turned round again in front of the mirror, so that he should seem to be looking at his grand things.

The cat chamberlains who were to carry the train stooped and pretended to lift it from the ground with both hands, and they walked along with their hands in the air. They dared not let it appear that they could not see anything.

Then the Cat Emperor walked along in the procession under the gorgeous canopy, and everybody in the streets and at the windows exclaimed, "How beautiful the Cat Emperor's new clothes are! What a splendid train! And they fit to perfection!" Nobody would let it appear that he could see nothing, for then he would not be fit for his post, or else he was a fool.

None of the Cat Emperor's clothes had been so successful before.

"But he has got nothing on," said a little kitten.

"Oh, listen to the innocent," said its father. And one cat whispered to the other what the kitten had said. "He has nothing on—a kitten says he has nothing on!"

"But he has nothing on!" at last cried all the cats.

The Cat Emperor writhed, for he knew it was true. But he thought "The procession must go on now." So he held himself stiffer than ever, tail high in the air, and the cat chamberlains held up the invisible train.

If man could be crossed with a cat, it would improve man, but it would deteriorate the cat.

Mark Twain

"Epitaph on the Duchess of Maine's Cat"

La Mothe le Vayer (1588-1672)

If nobility is earned, cats pay their dues in full. This poem describes the glorious afterlife and legacy in every cat's future, even if they must live nine lives to reach it.

Puss passer-by, within this simple tomb
Lies one whose life fell Atropos hath shred;
The happiest cat on earth hath heard her doom,
And sleeps for ever in a marble bed.
Alas! what long delicious days I've seen!
O cats of Egypt, my illustrious sires,
You who on altars, bound with garlands green,
Have melted hearts, and kindled fond desires,
Hymns in your praise were paid, and offerings too,
But I'm not jealous of those rights divine,
Since Ludovisa loved me, close and true,
Your ancient glory was less proud than mine.
To live a simple pussy by her side
Was nobler far than to be deified.

"Three Tabbies"

Kate Greenaway (1846-1901)

Three tabbies took out their cats to tea,
As well-behaved tabbies as well could be:
Each sat in the chair that each preferred,
They mewed for their milk, and they sipped and purred.
Now tell me this (as these cats you've seen them)—
How many lives had these cats between them?

6

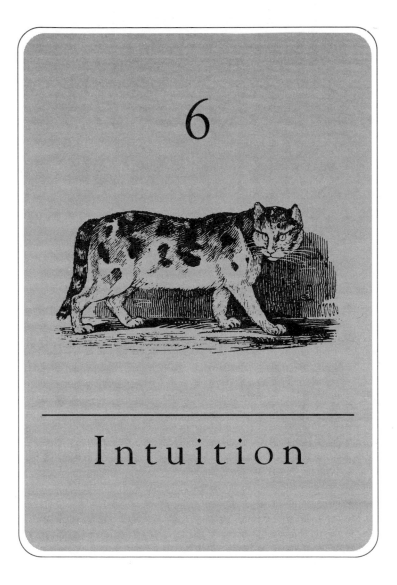

Intuition

The cat's sixth sense might be the reason it has nine lives. Cat authority Roger A. Caras summed it up best when he wrote: "Cats seem to know the punch lines of life."

Cats, indeed, seem to know what's around each corner before they turn it. Maybe it's because they spend time sitting still, absorbing their environment, while we caretakers rush about. They are calm, wise, and cryptic. Cats can sit motionless, and still seem a step ahead.

Tiffany, a Persian mix, was trapped by the January 1994 Los Angeles earthquake and found alive forty-one days later in the storage closet where she hid during the quake. According to Reuter News Service, Tiffany's owner, Laurie Booth, never gave up on finding the feline, posting neighborhood signs and advertising in the newspaper. Tiffany sensed her owner was a few yards away, and held out. The once eight-pound cat weighed just four pounds when she was discovered.

There are hundreds of such stories. I have a friend whose cat saw her mother faint one night and then ran to my friend's room to wake her. She calls Besa "the nurse."

The cat's poker face adds to our impression of their intuitive nature. With a face that shows no emotion, nearly every ounce of feeling is channeled through a cat's eyes: Narrow pupils are a sign of a nearby threat, while wide eyes mean he is ready to do battle. Often these reactions have more to do with what a cat senses than what he sees.

Throughout history, the intuitive nature of cats has been so revered that it's resulted in a number of superstitions. Cats have even been believed capable of bringing good luck or bad luck, and even of predicting the weather!

Watch a cat when it enters a room for the first time. It searches and smells about, it is not quiet for a moment, it trusts nothing until it has examined and made acquaintance with everything.

Jean-Jacques Rousseau (1712-1778)

"To a Cat"

Algernon Charles Swinburne (1837-1909)

A cat is a friend of "loftier" mind, empathizing with his caretaker, and knowing, without showing.

I

Stately, kindly, lordly friend,
  Condescend
Here to sit by me, and turn
Glorious eyes that smile and burn,

Golden eyes, love's lustrous meed,
On the golden page I read.
All your wondrous wealth of hair,
  Dark and fair,
Silken-shaggy, soft and bright
As the clouds and beams of night,
Pays my reverent hand's caress
Back with friendlier gentleness.

Dogs may fawn on all and some
  As they come;
You, a friend of loftier mind,
Answer friends alone in kind.
Just your foot upon my hand
Softly bids it understand.

Morning round this silent sweet
  Garden-seat
Shed its wealth of gathering light,
Thrills the gradual clouds with might,
Changes woodland, orchard, heath,
Lawn, and garden there beneath.

Fair and dim they gleamed below:
  Now they glow
Deep as even your sunbright eyes,
Fair as even the wakening skies.
Can it not or can it be
Now that you give thanks to see?

May not you rejoice as I,
   Seeing the sky
Change to heaven revealed, and bid
Earth reveal the heaven it hid
All night long from stars and moon,
Now the sun sets all in tune?

What within you wakes with day
   Who can say?
All too little may we tell,
Friends who like each other well,
What might haply, if we might,
Bid us read our lives aright.

II

Wild on woodland ways your sires
   Flashed like fires;
Fair as flame and fierce and fleet
As with wings on wingless feet
Shone and sprang your mother, free,
Bright and brave as wind or sea.

Free and proud and glad as they,
   Here today
Rests or roams their radiant child,
Vanquished not, but reconciled,
Free from curb of aught above
Save the lovely curb of love.

Love through dreams of souls divine
   Fain would shine
Round a dawn whose light and song
Then should right our mutual wrong—
Speak, and seal the love-lit law
Sweet Assisi's seer foresaw.

Dreams were theirs; yet haply may
   Dawn a day
When such friends and fellows born,
Seeing our earth as fair at morn,
May for wiser love's sake see
More of heaven's deep heart than we.

"A Description of a City Shower" (1710)

Jonathan Swift

Many a weatherman surely envies the cat's intuition.

Careful observers may foretell the hour
(By sure prognostics) when to dread a shower;
While rain depends, the pensive cat gives o'er
Her frolics, and pursues her tail no more.

"The Cat and His Shadow"

Not only does the cat sense, but he senses the sensible, as retold in this classic fable.

A cat, with a mouse in his mouth, was crossing a brook. As he looked down into the smooth clear water, he saw his shadow there, and thought that it was another cat with a bigger mouse.

He contemplated dropping what he had to jump into the water and seize the bigger mouse, but at that moment he saw a dripping dog emerge from the brook, his mouth empty and marked by a sad frown.

Suddenly the cat was overwhelmed by an odd sense of déjà vu. He looked again at the bigger mouse, and then trotted off, content with his own catch.

The dog, who had lost all that he had, was obliged to go without dinner.

———

The intelligence of Calvin was something phenomenal, in his rank of life. He established a method of communicating his wants, and even some of his sentiments; and he could help himself in many things. There was a furnace register in a retired room, where he used to go when he wished to be alone, that he always opened when he desired more heat; but never shut it, any more than he shut a door after himself. . . . I hesitate a little to speak of his capacity for friendship and the affectionateness of his nature, for I know from his own reserve that he would not care to have it much talked about. We understood each other perfectly, but we never made any fuss about it; when I spoke his name and snapped my fingers, he came to me; when I returned home at night, he was pretty sure to be waiting for me near the gate, and would rise and saunter along the walk, as if his being there was purely accidental—so shy was he commonly of showing feeling. There was one thing he never did—he never rushed through an open doorway. He never forgot his dignity. If he had asked to have the door opened, and was eager to go out, he always went out deliberately; I can see him now, standing on the sill, looking about the sky as if he was thinking whether it were worthwhile to take an umbrella, until he was near having his tail shut in.

Charles Dudley Warner (1829-1900)

"The Cat and Aphrodite"

Aesop

A cat's intuition is a part of her makeup. In the following fable, Aesop shows no amount of desire can change this.

A cat fell in love with a handsome youth and begged Aphrodite to change her into a woman. The goddess, pitying her sad state, transformed her into a beautiful girl, and when the young man saw her he fell in love with her and took her home to be his wife. While they were resting in their bedroom, Aphrodite, who was curious to know if the cat's instincts had changed along with her shape, let a mouse loose in front of her. She at once forgot where she was, leapt up from the bed, and ran after the mouse to eat it. The indignant goddess then restored her to her original form.

Moral: A bad man retains his character even if his outward appearance is altered.

A cat shows more of its breeding through its eyes than it does through any other feature.

Louis Wain, 19th Century

---

from Gulliver's Travels

Jonathan Swift (1667-1745)

In the midst of dinner, my mistress's favorite cat leaped into her lap. I heard a noise behind me like that of a dozen stocking weavers at work. Turning my head, I found it proceeded from the purring of this animal, who seemed to be three times larger than an ox, as I computed by the view of her head, and one of her paws, while her mistress was feeding and stroking her. The fierceness of this creature's countenance altogether discomposed me; though I stood at the farther end of the table, above fifty feet off, and although my mistress held her fast for fear she might give a spring and seize me in her talons. But it happened there was no danger; for the cat took not the least notice of me when my master placed me within three yards of her. And as I have been always told, and found true by experience in my travels, that flying or displaying fear before a fierce animal is a certain way to make it pursue or attack you, so I resolved in this dangerous juncture to show no manner of concern. I walked with intrepidity five or six times before the very head of the cat, and came within half a yard of her; whereupon she drew herself back, as if she were more afraid of me.

The Persian Princess
and the Pea

The sensitive nature of felines ranges from alley cat to aristocat.

There was once a cat prince, and he wanted to marry a princess, but she had to be a real princess. He traveled the world over to find one, but there was always something wrong. He couldn't really put his finger on it, but his intuition told him none of those he encountered were quite right. Tired and disappointed, he returned to his palace.

Not long after his return, on a grumbling, stormy night, rain poured down and lightning flashed. There was a loud knocking on the door, and the old cat king, the prince's father, opened it. In the driving rain, who should be standing there but a Persian cat—a princess, or so she claimed. Her strawberry blonde fur hung limp and dripping wet, and her clothes, apparently once fine garments, were tattered. She maintained, however, that she *was* a real princess.

"We'll soon see," the old queen murmured to herself. And she went to the extra bedroom, took off all the sheets and blankets, and put a little pea on the bedstead. She stacked twenty more mattresses on top, and put twenty eider-downs upon the mattresses. This is where the Persian princess would sleep.

The queen told her husband and son what she had done, and the next morning, when the Persian kitty came down for breakfast, they all three observed her closely.

"Excuse me, kitten, but how was your night? Did you sleep well?"

The princess looked at them with tired eyes and puffy jowls and said, "I'm sorry to say, but it was a wretched night. I hardly slept at all. My bed felt hard and lumpy. I'm black and blue all over."

The prince smiled broadly. It was plain that the Persian kitty was truly a princess. Her intuition was so keen she sensed a pea through twenty mattresses and twenty eiderdowns. Only a princess would have been so sensitive.

The cat prince was overjoyed and soon made her his wife. He knew it was right.

7

Honesty

Cats make no apologies for who they are, what they want, or how they act. They will not cower with sad eyes and a forgive-me face when a vase tumbles to the floor from a shelf they've been traversing. They are what they are, and they do what they do.

Cats are emotionally tactless, which is not to say they do not love. But they cannot pretend affection for everyone they meet. And they will not stay in a room long enough to explain their feelings.

To humans this might sound simply rude, but we could actually learn much from a cat's honesty. People engage in back stabbing and two-faced fawning. The cat does not dispense emotion when it is not felt. Felines will not expend the time or trouble on deceit.

The pampered pussy, spoiled worse than many children, honestly believes she deserves it. The tomcat, shuffling along alleys and digging in trash, likewise sees nothing wrong with his lifestyle.

If honesty among humans is a highly esteemed virtue, why does the cat's innate honesty often rub many people the wrong way?

from "On the Death of a Favorite Cat, Drowned in a Tub of Gold Fishes"

Thomas Gray

Her conscious tail her joy declared;
The fair round face, the snowy beard,
The velvet of her paws,
Her coat, that with the tortoise vies,
Her ears of jet, and emerald eyes,
She saw; and purred applause.

———

The trouble with cats is that they've got no tact.

P. G. Wodehouse (1881-1975)

———

Cats seem to go on the principle that it never does any harm to ask for what you want.

Joseph Wood Krutch (1893-1970)

from Alice's Adventures in Wonderland

Lewis Carroll (1832-1898)

You might not like what they have to say, but cats will never deceive you.

The Cat only grinned when it saw Alice. It looked good-natured, she thought: still it had *very* long claws and a great many teeth, so she felt that it ought to be treated with respect.

"Chessire Puss," she began, rather timidly, as she did not at all know whether it would like the name: however, it only grinned a little wider. "Come, it's pleased so far," thought Alice, and she went on. "Would you tell me, please, which way I ought to go from here?"

"That depends a good deal on where you want to go," said the Cat.

"I don't much care where—" said Alice.

"Then it doesn't matter which way you go," said the Cat.

"—so long as I get *somewhere*," Alice added as an explanation.

"Oh, you're sure to do that," said the Cat, "if you only walk long enough."

Alice felt that this could not be denied, so she tried another question. "What sort of people live about here?"

"In *that* direction," the Cat said, waving its right paw round, "lives a Hatter: and in *that* direction," waving the other paw, "lives a March Hare. Visit either you like: they're both mad."

"But I don't want to go among mad people," Alice remarked.

"Oh, you can't help that," said the Cat. "We're all mad here. I'm mad. You're mad."

"How do you know I'm mad?" said Alice.

"You must be," said the Cat, "or you wouldn't have come here."

———————

The Ugly Kitten

Perhaps the reason there are so many strays is that cats cannot lie to themselves about anything. Instead, they search. In this case not for belonging, but for honest contentment.

Once a mother cat gave birth to six kittens. The first five were perfect little pussycats all, white with tiny pink tongues. The last kitten took its time coming into the world. And when it did, the mother cat miaowed in displeasure.

"My what an ugly kitten," she said of the yellow and blackish-brown, striped fur ball with its baggy coat of fur.

The mother cat set out in the meadow, her brood trailing behind her. The ugly kitten tottered along, last in line. "At least it can walk," the mother cat said.

She took her new family to a barnyard, where she wanted to introduce them to the other cats and animals she knew.

"Mind your manners, children," she said. "Say 'Miaow' just as I have taught you and keep your tails high and proud."

The other animals in the barnyard voiced great approval of the kittens. "Oh, but look at that terrible little kitten!" hissed one cat. He began to snip and growl at the newborn in ridicule.

"Let him be," said his mother. "He is doing no harm."

"He's so queer, I have to peck him," said an eagle, and soon all the animals in the barn were taunting the kitten and his fur that stood on end in some places and was matted in others. Even his brothers and sisters began making fun of him.

This went on for days, and then weeks, till the kitten was at wit's end. One afternoon, when the barnyard animals were teasing relentlessly, he ran away over the hill and through the meadow. His little legs tired not long after he began his escape, and he longed to stop. But there were still plenty of animals making great fun of him.

"What sort of creature are you?" asked a zebra. "You are certainly frightfully ugly!"

He continued to walk alone. One of the elephants approached him.

"I say, ugly creature, I think we are taking a fancy to you. Come run with us."

But just then a loud "Bang! Bang!" rang out. Hunters were shooting at the big gray beasts and they stampeded off. The kitten ran off, terrified.

He came to a series of bungalows, and slipped through a crack in one. A woman, a cat, and a hen sat in the room.

"What on earth is that?" asked the woman.

"A very strange creature," said the cat.

"Can you lay eggs?" asked the hen.

"No," said the poor little kitten.

"Can you purr?" asked the cat.

"No," the kitten replied truthfully.

"Then what use are you?" snapped the cat.

"Not much," thought the kitten, and he scurried out of the house and took refuge near a pond. "If I had lied, maybe they would have wanted me to live with them. But then I wouldn't be able to live with myself."

The summer passed slowly. The grass turned from green to brown, and leaves danced in the wind. The sky grew cold and gray. One evening, near sunset, the kitten heard a great rumbling. He hid behind a rock and watched a herd of great tigers come to a stop to drink from the water. They were a majestic sight with golden coats and black stripes and deep, intense eyes. The kitten had never admired any animal as much.

One of the largest tigers suddenly let out a multipitched roar that began deep and floated up, echoing off the trees. The herd rumbled off again. As they did, the kitten let out his own strange roar, and he longed to run with such an impressive group.

He dreamed of those tigers all winter, using his thoughts to warm his shivering little shape. One day a man came to ice fish at the pond, found the icy kitten, and carried him home.

"What a nice little plaything!" cried his children, and they ran to pick him up. But the kitten was so afraid of every creature he met he thought that the children would hurt him. In his fright, he bumped into the milk pan and sent milk spurting up all over the floor and the room. The woman let out a loud shriek, and the kitten, even more frightened, ran into the butter cask then in and out of the meal tub. The woman ran for the tongs, intending to hit the wild creature, and the children fell over each other chasing the kitten in noisy laughter.

The kitten scampered out the door.

All winter long he lived alone in bitter cold. By and by, birds returned, and the sun began to shine again. The kitten found himself in a field of long green grasses, and across the way he could see the tigers, the stately cats he so admired.

The eagles overhead cried out, "Look! The tigers are back," and many animals ran to greet the beasts.

"I will run to them, too," the kitten thought, "even though they will likely taunt and pummel me." He began striding toward the tigers where they drank from a big pond.

When he reached the water they turned and started toward him. He bent down to meet their attack. But when he did, he saw his own reflection for the first time. He was no longer an ugly kitten. He was still golden and blackish-brown, but he had finally grown into his baggy coat. He was taut and striped and majestic and beautiful! He, himself, was a tiger!

The other tigers approached not to taunt, but to welcome him. They strutted around him, praising their new companion's handsome looks. The eagles spread the word: "There is a splendid young tiger at the drinking pool. He'll be the toast of these plains!"

"How happy I am," thought the kitten. "I never even dreamed that I could be so happy when I was the ugly kitten. It doesn't matter the least having been born in a litter of strays if one looks honestly for where he best belongs."

Cats, you see, do not possess a capacity to be anything but what they are.

He can talk but insolently says nothing.
What of it?
When one is frank, one's very presence
is a compliment.

Marianne Moore (1887-1972)

————

"The Little Cat Angel"

Leontine Stanfield

Kittens are especially upfront. They are unaccustomed to
cunning and don't see the need for deceit.

> The ghost of a little white kitten
> Crying mournfully, early and late,
> Distracted St. Peter, the watchman,
> As he guarded the heavenly gate.
> "Say, what do you mean," said his Saintship,
> "Coming here and behaving like that?"
> "I want to see Nellie, my missus,"
> Sobbed the wee little ghost of a cat.
> "I know she's not happy without me,
> Won't you open and let me go in?"
> "Begone," gasped the horrified watchman,
> "Why, the very idea is a sin;
> I open the gate to good angels,
> Not to stray little kittens like you."

"All right," mewed the little white kitten,
"Though a cat, I'm a good angel, too."
Amazed at so bold an assertion,
But aware he must make no mistake,
In silence St. Peter long pondered,
For his name and repute were at stake;
Then placing the cat in his bosom,
With a "Whist now, and say all your prayers,"
He opened the heavenly portals
And ascended the bright golden stairs.
A little girl angel came flying,
"That's my kitty, St. Peter," she cried,
And seeing the joy of their meeting,
Peter let the cat angel abide.

This tale is the tale of a kitten
Dwelling now with the blessed above;
It vanquished grim Death and High Heaven,
For the name of the kitten was Love.

"Pussy-Cat and Queen"

Mother Goose

"Pussy Cat, Pussy Cat, where have you been?"
"I've been to London to look at the queen."
"Pussy Cat, Pussy Cat, what did you there?"
"I frightened a little mouse under her chair."

I suspect that many an ailurophobe hates cats only because he feels they are better people than he is—more honest, more secure, more loved, more whatever he is not.

Winifred Carriere
Twentieth Century American writer

A cat has "absolute emotional honesty: human beings, for one reason or another, may hide their feelings, but a cat does not."

Ernest Hemingway

The Mouse Who Cried Cat

For cats and humans alike, lest we forget, honesty is always the best policy.

There was a mouse who kept watch over his large family from the edge of their little village. Once he thought he would play a trick on the villagers and have some fun at their expense. So he ran toward the mouse village crying out with all his might:

"Cat! Cat! Come and help! The cat is on his way!"

The mice left their work and ran to the mouse's post, but when they got there the mouse laughed at them for their panic; there was no cat there.

Still another day the mouse tried the same trick, and the mice came running to help and again the prankster laughed at them.

Then one day a cat did approach the village and began eating their winter stores. In a great fright, the mouse began to scream, "Cat! Cat! There is a cat in the village! Help!"

The cat's reaction was to chuckle. "Poor mouse, your dishonesty is going to be the end of you. You teased and tricked, and now no one will believe you. And *that* is the honest truth."

The mice in the village did hear their guard, but they thought it was another mean trick. No one paid the least attention, or went near him, and the mouse lost his life, as did several of his relatives.

8

Loyalty

Theirs is not a lick-your-face, drag-you-from-a-fire, till-death-do-us-part loyalty. It's much more subtle, and is almost always a two-way street.

With cats, as with people, loyalty is laden with expectations. Do for me, and I'll think about doing for you. Try and dress me up in doll clothes and my claws will pop out of the frilly sleeve. Let me sleep ten hours a day, and I'll curl up on your lap once every so often.

A dear friend of mine lived with her cat before she lived with her husband. Winker now wakes them both about 4:00 A.M. each day with incessant miaowing and has to be taken to another room; however, for the three months my friend's husband spent on a military maneuver in Somalia, Winker didn't sack out on the foot of the bed. He crept around at night, hissing at doors and windows, occasionally coming to rest near her head. Winker abandoned his customary 4:00 A.M. retreat. "My protector," she called him. Recently, the couple returned from a trip, and my friend got a purred "Welcome," her husband a hissed "Who cares."

Cats, in their own way, take care of their caretakers. But any mention of their loyalty wouldn't be complete without mentioning the reciprocal devotion of cat owners. They will spoon-feed baby food to their cats who fall ill, go to great lengths to give them stuffed Christmas stockings, and buy assorted cat paraphernalia to show their own loyalty.

In 1994, Carol Ann Timmel sued Tower Air to force a thorough search of the jumbo jet on which her cat Tabitha had escaped from a carrier. The story, which made national headlines, had a happy ending when, after twelve days and thirty-two thousand miles of traveling, Tabitha loyally answered her owner's call.

For many, cats are not merely loyal pets. They are a way of life. In 1993, an eleven-year-old Turkish Angora cat from Seattle named Tinker inherited an estate valued at $500,000 that provided for a live-in caretaker, grooming, and medical bills for the rest of its life. Enough said.

---

from Inquiries into Human Faculty, 1883

Francis Galton

The cat is the only non-gregarious domestic animal. It is retained by its extraordinary adhesion to the comforts of the house in which it is reared.

"Little Pussy"

Mother Goose

I like little Pussy
 Her coat is so warm,
And if I don't hurt her
 She'll do me no harm;
So I'll not pull her tail,
 Nor drive her away,
But Pussy and I
 Very gently will play.

---

from "The Kitten"

Joanna Baillie (1762-1851)

Being loyal does not mean being subservient. Cats, and
especially Baillie's kitten, are all over the place. But when
it counts, they're on your side.

Wanton droll, whose harmless play
Beguiles the rustic's closing day,
When, drawn the evening fire about,
Sit aged crone and thoughtless lout,
And child upon his three-foot stool,
Waiting until his supper cool,

And maid, whose cheek outblooms the rose,
As bright the blazing faggot glows,
Who bending to the friendly light,
Plies her task with busy sleight;
Come, show the tricks and sportive graces,
Thus circled round with merry faces!
Backward coil'd and crouching low,
With glaring eyeballs watch thy foe,
The housewife's spindle whirling round,
Or thread, or straw, that on the ground
Its shadow throws, by urchin sly
Held out to lure thy roving eye;
Then stealing onward, fiercely spring
Upon the tempting, faithless thing.
Now whirling round with bootless skill,
Thy bo-peep tail provokes thee still,
As still beyond thy curving side
Its jetty tip is seen to glide;
Till from thy centre starting far,
Thou sidelong veer'st with rump in air
Erected stiff, and gait awry,
Like madam in her tantrums high;
Though ne'er a madam of them all,
Whose silken kirtle sweeps the hall,
More varied trick and whim displays
To catch the admiring stranger's gaze.
Doth power in measured verses dwell,
All thy vagaries wild to tell?
Ah, no! the start, the jet, the bound,
The giddy scamper round and round,
With leap and toss and high curvet,

And many a whirling somerset
(Permitted by the modern Muse
Expression technical to use),
These mock the deftest rhymester's skill,
But poor in art, though rich in will.
The featest tumbler, stage bedight,
To thee is but a clumsy wight,
Who every limb and sinew strains
To do what costs thee little pains;
For which, I trow, the gaping crowd
Requites him oft with plaudits loud.
But, stopp'd the while thy wanton play,
Applauses too thy pains repay:
For then beneath some urchin's hand
With modest pride thou tak'st thy stand,
While many a stroke of kindness glides
Along thy back and tabby sides.
Dilated swells thy glossy fur,
And loudly croons thy busy purr,
As, timing well the equal sound,
Thy clutching feet bepat the ground,
And all their harmless claws disclose
Like prickles of an early rose,
While softly from thy whisker'd cheek
Thy half-closed eyes peer, mild and meek.
But not alone by cottage fire
Do rustics rude thy feats admire.
The learned sage, whose thoughts explore
The widest range of human lore,
Or with unfetter'd fancy fly
Through airy heights of poesy,

Pausing, smiles with alter'd air
To see thee climb his elbow-chair,
Or, struggling on the mat below,
Hold warfare with his slipper'd toe.
The widow'd dame, or lonely maid,
Who, in the still, but cheerless shade
Of home unsocial, spends her age,
And rarely turns a letter'd page,
Upon her hearth for thee lets fall
The rounded cork, or paper ball,
Nor chides thee on thy wicked watch,
The ends of ravell'd skein to catch,
But lets thee have thy wayward will,
Perplexing oft her better skill.
E'en he, whose mind of gloomy bent,
In lonely tower, or prison pent,
Reviews the coil of former days,
And loathes the world and all its ways;
What time the lamp's unsteady gleam
Hath roused him from his moody dream,
Feels, as thou gambol'st round his seat,
His heart of pride less fiercely beat,
And smiles, a link in thee to find,
That joins it still to living kind.

"My Kitten"

Mother Goose

Hey, my kitten, my kitten,
And hey, my kitten, my deary!
Such a sweet pet as this
Was neither far nor neary.

———

Snow White and the Seven Cats

We should all be so lucky to have friends who'll pull us out of scrapes. Many cat lovers claim their pets have saved them in oh-so sticky situations.

Long ago there lived a king and queen who had a beautiful daughter. Her skin was white as snow, her hair was as black as ebony, and her lips were as red as blood. She was called Snow White.

When she was young, her mother died and her father, the king, took another wife. The new queen was a very vain woman and could not bear the thought that someone was prettier than she. She often looked into a magic mirror and said:

"Mirror, mirror on the wall,
Who is the fairest one of all?"

The mirror would say back:

"You, oh Queen, are the fairest in the land."

The queen knew the mirror to tell her only the truth. So she was angry when one day she asked the mirror:

"Mirror, mirror on the wall,
Who is the fairest one of all?"

And the mirror replied:

"You, oh Queen, are fair, 'tis true,
But Snow White is now fairer than you."

The queen was quite angry, and ordered a huntsman to kill her stepdaughter. He obediently took Snow White to the forest and took out his knife, but could not actually kill her. He allowed her to run away into the woods.

She ran and ran, until she came to a small house. Inside, she saw a meal for seven prepared. She was hungry after her adventure in the woods, so she ate some food and then fell asleep.

That night, the owners of the little house returned. They were seven cats who dug for gold and diamonds in the hills nearby. They were struck by Snow White's beauty, but respecting a good nap, agreed not to wake her.

In the morning, she woke by herself and told the hospitable cats her story. They invited her to stay on as long as necessary. And she did.

Meanwhile, the wicked queen again spoke to her mirror:

"Mirror, mirror on the wall,
Who is the fairest one of all?"

And the mirror replied:

"You, oh Queen, are fair 'tis true,
But Snow White, living with the seven cats,
Is fairer than you."

The queen fumed with anger and decided to visit the cats' house dressed as an old peddler woman with a basket of things to sell. She arrived and knocked on the door.

Snow White answered, and the wicked queen sold her a silk tie for her dress. She offered to help tie it, and she pulled it so tight that Snow White could hardly breathe and she fainted.

The seven cats arrived home and rushed to Snow White's side, loosening the dress cord. The queen, meanwhile, returned to her mirror:

"Mirror, mirror, on the wall,
Who is the fairest one of all?"

And the mirror repeated,

"You, oh Queen, are fair, 'tis true,
But Snow White, living with the seven cats,
Is fairer than you."

The queen's rage boiled. And she concocted a poisoned comb and returned to the cats' house.

"Go away, I won't let anyone in!" yelled Snow White.

"Just look at this lovely comb!" said the queen, who was again dressed as an old peddler.

Snow White leaned out of the window, and in an instant, the wicked queen stuck the poisoned comb in her hair and again caused Snow White to faint.

Again the cats returned to their friend, and pulled the comb out to relieve her. And again the queen learned from her mirror that she was not the fairest in the land. With a vengeance, the wicked woman vowed to make sure her next trip was her last.

The next morning the queen dressed as a village girl and carried a big basket of red apples. She knocked at the cats' door, calling, "Ripe apples! Big juicy apples!"

"What's the matter?" asked the queen. "You seem scared that I might poison you. The apples are so sweet. Look, I'll even take the first bite."

She took a bite from the green half of the apple, and handed it to Snow White, who thought it must be fine to eat.

But she nibbled from the red half, and fell down as if dead.

With an evil laugh, the queen returned to her mirror:

"Mirror, mirror on the wall,
Who is the fairest one of all?"

This time the mirror replied:

"You, oh Queen, are the fairest in the land."

The seven cats found Snow White lying on the floor but could not rouse her. They miaowed loudly and even licked her hands. For three days and nights the loyal cats screeched loudly over her, their way of crying. Finally, they laid her in a glass coffin so that everyone could see her.

Eventually, a prince came riding by. He took one look at Snow White and proclaimed his love, begging the cats to let him take her back to his palace. The cats respected his perseverence, and agreed to let him take her.

The prince's servants began to carry the coffin away, but doing so jarred a piece of poison apple from her throat. She opened her eyes and sat up, bewildered.

"Where am I?" she asked.

"You are with me, thanks to these loyal cats," said the prince. "Please come to my palace and be my wife."

Snow White accepted, but said she wanted to bring her dedicated cat friends with her, so that they might enjoy a life of luxury as a reward for their care.

On the very day of the wedding, the wicked queen spoke to her mirror:

"Mirror, mirror on the wall,
Who is the fairest one of all?"
And she got unexpected news:
"You, oh Queen, are fair, 'tis true,
But Snow White, the prince's bride and the
cats' keeper
Is fairer than you."
The queen was so mad that she dropped dead of anger.
Snow White, the prince, and the cats lived happily ever after.

"The Cat's Prayer"

Belgian traditional

O my Master,
Do not expect me to be your slave, I have a thirst for freedom.
Do not probe my secret thoughts, I have a love of mystery.
Do not smother me with caresses, I have a preference for reserve.
Do not humiliate me, I have a sense of pride.
Do not, I beg, abandon me, I have a sure fidelity.
I'll return your love for me, I have a sense of true devotion.

from Pudd'nhead Wilson
1894

Mark Twain

Is a home really a home without a cat? Twain is as loyal to
his feline friends as they are to him.

A home without a cat—and a well-fed, well-petted and properly revered cat—may be a perfect home, perhaps, but how
can it prove title?

9

Playfulness

All work and no play will never make the cat a dull animal. For cats, work is a foreign concept; playing and living are synonymous. I know what you're thinking. *That's a virtue? If the cat isn't industrious, what's the lesson there?*

I suggest it's a lesson in priorities. How often does work prevent us from enjoying life? I don't mean the kind of work that pays the electric bill and puts food on the table. I mean the unnecessary mental labor that causes us to miss life's simple pleasures. A cat would never pass up the chance for a nap in the sunlight, or a race with a butterfly. Humans are usually too busy cleaning the dirty windows to notice the sunlight. And in their race from place to place, they never even see the butterflies.

Maybe scratching doors and getting tangled in yarn isn't exciting to us, but when's the last time you saw an adult swinging in the park? Or walking in the rain? Those few who do quite possibly learned such lessons from their free-spirited cats.

Frivolous? Silly? Perhaps. But consider what such playfulness does for the cat's disposition. They live lighter. They absorb more. They enjoy more. They are not necessarily happier, but they have a sense of perspective. If we could stay unwound like cats do, we might all just live to 210!

from "The Robber Kitten"

Anonymous

One day it met a robber dog
And they sat down to drink;
The dog did laugh, and joke, and sing,
Which made the kitten wink,
Wink, wink wink,
Which made the kitten wink!

―――――――

"The Owl and the Pussycat"

Edward Lear (1812-1888)

Lear's pea green boat was a wonderful playground for
the pussycat in this tale.

The Owl and the Pussy-Cat went to sea
In a beautiful pea-green boat;
They took some honey and plenty of money
Wrapped up in a five-pound note.
The Owl looked up to the stars above,
And sang to a small guitar,
"O lovely Pussy, O Pussy, my love,
What a beautiful Pussy you are,
          You are,
          You are!

What a beautiful Pussy you are!"
Pussy said to the Owl, "You elegant fowl,
How charmingly sweet you sing!
Oh! let us be married; too long have we tarried:
But what shall we do for a ring?"
They sailed away, for a year and a day,
To the land where the bong-tree grows;
And there in a wood, a Piggy-wig stood,
With a ring at the end of his nose,
   His nose,
   His nose,
With a ring at the end of his nose.

"Dear Pig, are you willing to sell for one shilling
Your ring?" Said the Piggy, "I will."
So they took it away, and were married next day
By the Turkey who lives on the hill.
They dined on mince and slices of quince,
Which they ate with a runcible spoon;
And hand in hand, on the edge of the sand,
They danced by the light of the moon,
   The moon,
   The moon,
They danced by the light of the moon.

———

What fun to be a cat!

Christopher Morley (1890-1957)

One of them likes to be crammed into a corner-pocket of the billiard table—which he fits as snugly as does a finger in a glove and then he watches the game (and obstructs it) by the hour, and spoils many a shot by putting out his paw and changing the direction of a passing ball. Whenever a ball is in his arms, or so close to him that it cannot be played upon with risk of hurting him, the player is privileged to remove it to one of the three spots that chances to be vacant.

Samuel L. Clemens, in a letter

———

A cat came fiddling out of a barn
With a pair of bagpipes under her arm;
She could sing nothing but fiddle-de-dee,
The mouse has married the bumblebee;
Pipe, cat—dance, mouse—
We'll have a wedding at our good house.

Mother Goose

———

Placing the kitten
To weigh her on the balance . . .
She went on playing.

Issa (1763-1827)

There is nothing in the animal world, to my mind, more delightful than grown cats at play. They are so swift, and light and graceful, so subtle and designing, and yet so richly comic.

Monica Edwards

---

from "The Kitten and Falling Leaves"

William Wordsworth (1770-1850)

Fall foliage brings out the playfulness in people and animals alike. What a pity that spirit eventually leaves us.

That way look, my Infant, lo!
What a pretty baby-show!
See the Kitten on the wall,
Sporting with the leaves that fall,
Withered leaves—one—two—and three—
From the lofty elder-tree!
Through the calm and frosty air
Of this morning bright and fair,
Eddying round and round they sink
Softly, slowly: one might think,
From the motions that are made,
Every little leaf conveyed
Sylph or Faery hither tending,—

To this lower world descending,
Each invisible and mute,
In his wavering parachute.
—But the Kitten, how she starts,
Crouches, stretches, paws, and darts!
First at one, and then its fellow,
Just as light and just as yellow;
There are many now—now one—
Now they stop and there are none:
What intenseness of desire
In her upward eye of fire!
With a tiger-leap half-way
Now she meets the coming prey,
Lets it go as fast, and then
Has it in her power again:
Now she works with three or four
Like an Indian conjurer;
Quick as he in feats of art,
Far beyond in joy of heart.
Were her antics played in the eye
Of a thousand standers-by,
Clapping hands with shout and stare,
What would little Tabby care
For the plaudits of the crowd?
Over happy to be proud,
Over wealthy in the treasure
Of her own exceeding pleasure! . . .

. . . Yet, whate'er enjoyments dwell
In the impenetrable cell
Of the silent heart which Nature

Furnishes to every creature;
Whatsoe'er we feel and know
Too sedate for outward show,
Such a light of gladness breaks,
Pretty Kitten! from thy freaks,—
Spreads with such a living grace
O'er my little Dora's face;
Yes, the sight so stirs and charms
Thee, Baby, laughing in my arms,
That almost I could repine
That your transports are not mine,
That I do not wholly fare
Even as ye do, thoughtless pair!
And I will have my careless season
Spite of melancholy reason,
Will walk through life in such a way
That, when time brings on decay,
Now and then I may possess
Hours of perfect gladsomeness.
—Pleased by any random toy:
By a kitten's busy joy,
Or an infant's laughing eye
Sharing in the ecstasy;
I would fare like that or this,
Find my wisdom in my bliss;
Keep the sprightly soul awake,
And have faculties to take,
Even from things by sorrow wrought,
Matter for a jocund thought,
Spite of care, and spite of grief,
To gambol with Life's falling Leaf.

Cats do not need to be shown how to have a good time, for they are unfailing ingenious in that respect.

James Mason

The City Cat and the Country Cat

Cats could work—if they found it fun!

Once upon a time, there was one little cat who lived in the country and there was another little cat who lived in the city. The country cat was very poor and he lived in a field and had to work very hard, but the city cat was very rich and he lived in a great big city house.

Well, one day the city cat, all dressed in his best city clothes, came to visit the country cat in his poor little home in the field.

"Why, my dear friend," said the city cat, seeing how the country cat lived. "How very poor you are."

"Yes, I suppose I'm poor," said the little country cat. "I haven't much to offer a friend, but if you'll make yourself comfortable, I'll go find you a mouse to eat."

So the city cat lay down lazily while the country cat went off and worked hard in the field, scampering after mice and dragging back some milk from his friend the cow. By and by he came home, happily exhausted from all his work. He was very satisfied and proud of the dinner he was bringing home to his friend.

"Is that all you have to eat?" the city cat turned up his nose. "All that work and nothing to show for your labor but a small mouse and a little puddle of milk! You should see how I live in the city—all the finest food to be had, and for no work at all. The cook in the house even makes cakes, and when no one is looking, I jump up on the counter and devour it. Hardly anyone gets angry. It's a frivolous life, so very fun. Come to town and see!"

And the country cat felt sorry for himself.

"I do work hard, and I have fun playing, but I do get little in return. It must be fun to lie around all day. I'll come to town."

So the two cats walked back to town until they came to the grandest house the country cat had ever seen. They scampered into the kitchen, where indeed, a freshly baked cake and a bottle of milk sat out.

"This is real living," the city cat said proudly. "Look at those goodies on the counter! What a meal!"

They were creeping up to the cake when bang! the kitchen door swung open and there appeared the face of the cook.

"Scat! Scat! You mangy cats!" The friends ran off into another room.

"We'll have another try in a moment," the city cat said to the country cat as they jumped upon a white sofa.

Within minutes, "Off, off, kitties! Do not dirty the furniture!" Again they ran away.

In another room, the hungry cats found a spool of ribbon and begin to unwind and scratch at it. "Don't touch that!" came an angry voice from the door.

The frustrated cats tried the kitchen again. The cake was gone, and a single, small bowl of dry cat food rested on a towel, in the corner.

The country cat smiled. "So this is your grand life in the city! You try to eat, and you get chased. You try to rest, and you get disturbed. And you try to play, and you get yelled at.

"Your life of play, my friend, is not very much fun. And you have no independence to be yourself. I'd far rather be able to have fun in the country than to be cooped up in the city."

He ran back to the country shouting, "Work that satisfies like play is better than no work at all."

"The Cat and the Fiddle"

Mother Goose

Hey, diddle, diddle, the cat and the fiddle,
The cow jumped over the moon;
The little dog laughed to see such sport,
While the dish ran away with the spoon.

Everything that moves serves to interest and amuse a cat.

F. A. Paradis de Moncrif (1687-1779)

Ten Little Kittens

Ten little kittens
running in line—
One went home
and then there were nine.

Nine little kittens
scratching on a gate—
One lost a claw
and then there were eight.

Eight little kittens
miaowing up to heaven—
One quieted down
and then there were seven.

Seven little kittens
playing little tricks—
One finished joking
and then there were six.

Six little kittens
teasing beehives—
One got stung
and then there were five.

Five little kittens
purring at the door—
One went around
and then there were four.

Four little kittens
climbed up a tree—
One slid down
and then there were three.

Three little kittens
untying a shoe—
One thought it smelled
and then there were two.

Two little kittens
stretching in the sun—
One fell asleep
and then there was one.

One little kitten
alone having fun—
He went into the house
and then there were none.

Acknowledgments

Many thanks to Jeff Guinn and Santa Claus, who I've grown to believe are truly related; my grandmother, Irl Neilon, who tried to instill in us a love of literature with two volumes of fairy tales in 1974; my mother, Mary Besze, who carries on that tradition and helped find the books twenty years later; Naomi Engel and her family of four; and Alicia and Brad Wanek—her affection and his coolness toward felines helped bridge the gaps.

Special thanks to Mike Towle and Jeanne Warren.

Resources

I am truly in awe of the wonderful, wide-ranging literature available on cats. Here are some of my favorites, many of which contain material found in this book. Every effort has been made to locate the copyright owners of material reproduced in this book. Omissions brought to our attention will be corrected in subsequent editions.

Altman, Roberta. *The Quintessential Cat*. New York: Macmillan, Inc., 1994.

Burden, Jean. *A Celebration of Cats*. New York: Paul S. Eriksson, Inc., 1974.

Caras, Roger A. *A Celebration of Cats*. New York: Simon and Schuster, 1986.

Carr, Samuel. *The Poetry of Cats*. New York: The Viking Press, Inc., 1975.

Foster, Dorothy. *In Praise of Cats: An Anthology*. New York: Crown Publishers, Inc., 1974.

Fox, Michael W. *Love is a Happy Cat*. Text copyright 1982 by Michael W. Fox. Reprinted by permission of Newmarket Press, 18 East 48 St., New York, New York 10017.

Gooden, Mona. *The Poets' Cat*. George G. Harrap & Co., Ltd., 1946.

Grimms' Fairy Tales by the Brothers Grimm. New York: Grosset & Dunlap, Inc., 1945.

Hamilton, Elizabeth. *Cats: A Celebration*. New York: Charles Scribner's Sons, 1979.

Herford, Oliver. *A Kitten's Garden of Verses*. Copyright 1911 by Oliver Herford, 1939 by Beatrice Herford Hayward. Used by permission of the publishers, Charles Scribner's Sons.

Jeans, Simon. *Book of Cat Names*. New York: Sterling Publishing Co., Inc., 1991.

Pitzer, Sara. *Cat Tales*. Copyright 1989 by Sara Pitzer. Used by permission of the publisher, August House, Inc., Little Rock, Arkansas.

The Real Mother Goose. New York: Macmillan, Inc. 1944.

Robbins, Maria Polushkin. *Puss in Books*. New York: Penguin Books USA, Inc., 1994.

Stillinger, Jack ed. *John Keats Complete Poems*. Cambridge, Mass.: The Belknap Press of Harvard University Press.

Suares, J. C. *Great Cats: The Who's Who of Famous Felines*. New York: Bantam Books, Inc., 1981.

Van Vechten, Carl. *The Tiger in the House*. Reprinted by permission of Alfred A. Knopf, Inc., 1920.

Wells, Carolyn and Louella D. Everett. *The Cat in Verse*. Miami: Granger Books, 1935, 1977.

Wood, Gerald L. *Animal Facts and Feats*. New York: Sterling Publishing Co., Inc., 1977.